A Study of Personal and Cultural Values

Culture, Mind, and Society

The Book Series of the Society for Psychological Anthropology

With its book series Culture, Mind, and Society and journal *Ethos*, the Society for Psychological Anthropology publishes innovative research in culture and psychology now emerging from the discipline of anthropology and related fields. As anthropologists seek to bridge gaps between ideation and emotion or agency and structure—and as psychologists, psychiatrists, and medical anthropologists search for ways to engage with cultural meaning and difference—this interdisciplinary terrain is more active than ever.

This book series from the Society for Psychological Anthropology establishes a forum for the publication of books of the highest quality that illuminate the workings of the human mind, in all of its psychological and biological complexity, within the social, cultural, and political contexts that shape thought, emotion, and experience.

Series Editor

Douglas Hollan, Department of Anthropology, University of California, Los Angeles

Editorial Board

Titles in the Series:

Adrie Kusserow, *American Individualisms: Child Rearing and Social Class in Three Neighborhoods*
Naomi Quinn, editor, *Finding Culture in Talk: A Collection of Methods*
Anna Mansson McGinty, *Becoming Muslim: Western Women's Conversions to Islam*
Roy D'Andrade, *A Study of Personal and Cultural Values: American, Japanese, and Vietnamese*

A Study of Personal and Cultural Values

American, Japanese, and Vietnamese

Roy D'Andrade

palgrave
macmillan

First published in 2008 by
PALGRAVE MACMILLAN™
175 Fifth Avenue, New York, N.Y. 10010 and
Houndmills, Basingstoke, Hampshire, England RG21 6XS
Companies and representatives throughout the world.

PALGRAVE MACMILLAN is the global academic imprint of the Palgrave Macmillan division of St. Martin's Press, LLC and of Palgrave Macmillan Ltd. Macmillan® is a registered trademark in the United States, United Kingdom and other countries. Palgrave is a registered trademark in the European Union and other countries.

ISBN-13: 978–0–230–60299–1
ISBN-10: 0–230–60299–1

Library of Congress Cataloging-in-Publication Data is available from the Library of Congress.

A catalogue record for this book is available from the British Library.

Design by Newgen Imaging Systems (P) Ltd., Chennai, India.

First edition: April 2008

10   9   8   7   6   5   4   3   2   1

Printed in the United States of America.

*This book is dedicated to Melford E. Spiro,
my teacher and friend for many years.*

Contents

List of Figures and Tables

Figures

Tables

Acknowledgments

I wish to acknowledge the help and assistance of April Leininger, Yasusuke Minami, Hidetada Shimizu, Jason Danely, Marcy Ronnenberg, Makoto Swane, James Boster, Kim Romney, and Shalom Schwartz as well as a number of research assistants who made this project possible. The support of the National Science Foundation is also gratefully acknowledged.

Chapter 1

Introduction—The Initial Puzzle

Both social scientists and ordinary people share a number of assumptions about values. For both, values are an essentializing concept. To say "Robert does not value honesty" is to claim that Robert lacks something deep and important which influences how he acts and feels. But if we just say that Robert tells lies, we are not necessarily making a deep attribution; it may be that Robert tells lies because he is an undercover FBI agent or because he is unusually tactful. Robert's lies may be explained by his role or his conduct under certain conditions; Robert's failure to value honesty, on the other hand, says something much more profound about him as a person.

While essentialization can be viewed as simplistic or reductive, essentializing terms are quite useful where there really is a strong causal force that causes some entity to have a certain nature (like genes). Essentializing terms such as *motive, trait,* and *schema* are the bread and butter of psychology. The concept *values* belongs to this family of terms. As values are essentializing constructs, they are important not just in psychology and the social sciences, but also in political discourse and ordinary talk.

Given agreement on the importance of values, one might expect that values would be among the most studied constructs in psychology and the social sciences. However, research on values has not been as extensive as research on motivation, or personality traits, or roles and institutions. There are exceptions; Weber, for example, was concerned with the whole question of the casual priority of self-interested motives in comparison to religious values. Parsons, much influenced by Weber, was a premier theorist of value. Parsonian theory treats values as central to the understanding of personality functioning, important in the integration of social systems and basic to the description of culture. Parsons was concerned with the internalization of values; the way values, especially moral values, from the cultural system become internal regulators of conduct and motivation (Parsons 1964). While lacking a theory of the process of internalization, Parsons pointed to the fact that while part of the regulation of human behavior comes from the rational anticipation of positive and negative sanctions, another major part comes from within, from the values of society that have become part of the superego.

For a short period of time, roughly between 1945 and 1955, value studies flourished in Harvard's department of Social Relations. Parsons was not the only eminent figure interested in values; Gordon Allport, a social psychologist and personality psychologist, made values a major concept in his theory of personality and the self. Allport carried out early research on prejudice, and on the process by which values are attributed to one group rather than another. He was also interested in the importance of values as a central part of the self (Allport 1960, Allport et al. 1966). The modern work by Shelley Taylor and other social psychologists on the importance of the affirmation of values in strengthening and affirming the self in the face of challenges and disaster is historically linked to Allport's work (Taylor and Brown 1988). Jerome Bruner, a cognitive psychologist, also used the concept of value in work on perception. Bruner found, for example, that a poor child sees a 50-cent piece as larger than the same-sized plain plastic disk The influence of values was part of what was called the "new look" in perception. Values influenced mental sets, and mental sets influenced perception (Bruner et al. 1956).

Parsons's ideas about values had a strong influence in anthropology through Kluckhohn and the Five Culture Study. The Five Culture Study was a comprehensive ethnographic research project which ran from 1948 to 1952 and was formed to study the values of Zuni, Mormon, Navaho, Spanish American, and Texan communities in the Ramah area of New Mexico. Kluckhohn, while disagreeing with Parsons about the degree to which the social system could be considered as separate from culture (D'Andrade 2006), did agree that values were of central concern both to the study of personality and the study of culture. Kluckhohn thought that the examination of five different cultures, all in the same geographical area, and under similar ecological constraints, would highlight the importance of values in creating cultural uniqueness (Edmonson 1973) As Kluckhohn phrased it, "Why do different value systems continue to exist in five cultures all having to meet similar problems of adjustment and survival in the same ecological area, all having been exposed by actual contact and by stimulus diffusion to each other's value ideas and practices?" (Kluckhohn 1951b, viii). Kluckhohn thought values were the answer and at first believed that the five culture study would be able to demonstrate this. As Kluckhohn said, "I am convinced that, if the essence of culture consists in patterned selectivity, this selectivity can be parsimoniously described and understood only if we are able to isolate and compare the key values that give different cultures each a distinctive quality" (Kluckhohn 1951b). The project had a distinguished list of contributors, including Evon Vogt, Florence Kluckhohn, Ethel Albert, Robert Bellah, John Roberts, A. K. Romney, Munro Edmonson, Fred Strodbeck, and many others (see the collected papers in *People of Rimrock: A Study of Values in Five Cultures*, Evon Z. Vogt and Ethel M. Albert, eds. 1966). A number of anthropologists and sociologists outside Harvard were also interested in values during this period, including John Gillin and George Spindler. Gillin (1955) was interested in American regional variations in values. His analysis, based on his reading and doing ethnography in the United States, was that Americans value *energy, pragmatism, cleanliness, novelty, optimism, individualism, competitiveness, fair play, cooperation, honesty, ability, recreation, efficiency,* and *moral self-regulation.* Regionally, for example, he proposed that in the Northeast the values of *hard work* and *thrift* were emphasized, while the Southeast emphasized *Protestant morality, white racism, regional chauvinism,* and *violence* as a solution for interpersonal and intergroup problems. Spindler, who developed a projective test for values, began his values work by analyzing the differences in values between mainline modern American and Native American cultures. Later he became interested in the changes in American values. According to his analysis, Americans were moving from achievement and individualistic values toward more group-oriented and interpersonally related orientations (Spindler 1955).

For a short period of time it looked as though values would prove central to the description and analysis of culture, society, and personality. But after the Five Culture Study, American anthropologists almost completely abandoned the study of values. So far as I know, Vogt, Roberts, Edmonson, Romney, Clyde Kluckhohn, and the other project researchers never again wrote about values or carried out research on values. While the importance of values continued to be stated in text-books, few empirical studies were published. Reading Ethel Albert's summary of the findings of the Five Culture Study in her introductory chapter to the papers in *The People of Rimrock,* one is impressed by the number and quality of publications produced by the project. However, something went wrong. No one built on the Five Culture Study and by the mid-1960s it was rarely taught in undergraduate classes or graduate seminars in anthropology.

In Albert's introductory chapter to *People of Rimrock* certain problems are mentioned that hint at the underlying impasse. She says,

"Some of the most acute methodological problems of the Values Study research appeared where they might have been least expected—at the seemingly elementary level of description and comparison." Albert goes on to discuss the problems involved in constructing a conceptual framework for values, and especially the problem of whether to use native concepts (the *emic* approach), or universalistic constructs developed by social scientists (the *etic* approach). She says both were used in the Five Culture Study, and the description of each value system aspired to report a *totality distinctive of each culture.*

No doubt the *etic-emic* problem did pose difficulties. But such difficulties were not unique to value studies. A rereading of the publications from the Five Culture Study leads to a different interpretation. The problem seems to be the assumption that culture could be characterized by a relatively small number of values. Contrast the study of values with the study of social structure. Most societies have a relatively small number of institutional role complexes: kinship role systems, political role systems, economic role systems, and religious role systems. In a simple society, the role system is based almost entirely on kinship with some secondary elaboration of political and religious roles. Although roles often involve a large number of norms, the number of roles in a tribal society tends to be small; sometimes in the dozens, rarely in the hundreds, never in the thousands. The relatively small number of roles makes it possible to describe the social structure of a society in a single monograph.

But values are not like this. There is no clear limit to the number of values. In any society, tribal or modern, there will be values concerning how people should treat each other, how the way people should work, the proper kinds of recreation, the correct relation to the supernatural, the best ways to relate to other societies, the best kinds of artifacts, how to socialize children, and so on. The problem becomes one of trying to organize many hundreds and even thousands of disparate items. As Evon Vogt (1955) said in his study of values in a small community of farmers in the Southwest that values may be treated as long lists ranging from the desirable ways of making houses or pottery to the desirable ways of worshiping the gods; every cultural feature has its value aspects (p. 7).

The Five Cultures Study began with a framework developed by Florence Kluckhohn (1950). This system was developed around universal human problems—the relation of man to man, of man to nature, of man to the supernatural, of man to activity, and of man to time. While none of the Five Culture Study participants directly criticized this framework, it was obvious that it was not sufficient to serve as a central coordinating construct for the wide range of data that had been collected. For example, in the Peoples of Rimrock, Florence Kluckhohn's organizing framework disappears entirely. Each chapter of the book, written by a separate author, organizes its description of values with respect to one of the traditional institutions of society: kinship, politics, religion, expressive activities (aesthetics, recreation), group relations, and so on. In these chapters values have no independent organizing principle; they are simply described *by reference to the institution to which they most directly pertain.*

The solution to the *etic-emic* problem Ethel Albert proposed in her introduction was the then new approach of ethnoscience that, she thought, would be able to uncover the structure of culture through linguistically oriented analysis. If, she speculated, the empirically oriented analytic methods of American ethnologists could discern this structure, this would make possible a purely cultural framework for values. Unfortunately, the idea of anything like a cultural grammar or structure was found to be hopelessly naive. Roger Keesing (1974) has said that the "notion of a 'cultural grammar' proved unproductive and inadequate in the face of the incredible richness of human knowledge and experience" (p. 78). Empirical investigation by a generation of ethnoscientists and cognitive anthropologists demonstrated that culture contains a huge number of cognitive and semantic structures, and that no one, two, or three structures characterize any culture (D'Andrade 1995). Culture never was a snowflake.

This left the study of cultural values without an organizing framework. So, while values stayed in the textbooks, the empirical study of values in anthropology languished. The radical turn in the late 1960s and 1970s, followed by postmodernism, made the study of values doubly otiose; why would anyone use a failed empirical approach when it did not work and was generally irrelevant to problems of inequality and epistemological critique? Not surprisingly, the value studies of the 1950s stopped almost entirely.

One exception was a study of Zinacantan values by Francesca Cancian (1975). Cancian's study was a study of values in which she collected and analyzed data concerning the things her respondents thought were *good.* Cancian's book is a fine ethnographic description of Highland Chiapas Mayan values. Cancian had expected that her value analysis would predict how Zinacantecos actually behave in a variety of situations. But after many failed behavioral predictions, her overall conclusion was that her respondents' standards concerning what is good were not reliable predictors of their real-world choices. Cancian argued that these results revealed a flaw in Parsonian theory, although Parsons would probably have responded that he had never thought that values were a major influence on *individual* decision making; values for him were most important as a means of integrating and legitimizing institutions (Lidz 1991, p. 32).

In psychology, systematic studies of values were also rare with the exception of work by Milton Rokeach (1973). Rokeach developed a questionnaire that contained a list of 36 value items which respondents were asked to rank with respect to how strongly the respondent endorsed each items. Rokeach's methods are discussed in chapter 3 and his findings are discussed in several of the chapters that follow. Many of the items found in standard value studies today go back to Rokeach's list of values, which included *equality, freedom, salvation, friendship, national security, a world at peace,* and so on. From the late 1960s to the 1980s, Rokeach carried out studies of value differences among different political parties and among different religious groups and occupations in the United States. The National Opinion Research Center administered the Rokeach value questionnaire over several years to large representative national samples.

In the 1990s, extensive value research was initiated by the social psychologist Shalom Schwartz (see Schwartz 2002). Schwartz added 22 new items to Rokeach's original list of 36 items. Respondents were asked to rate the importance of each item "as a guiding principle in my life." Data was collected from approximately 200 samples taken from 67 nations, encompassing in total more than 75,000 respondents. Schwartz's work is discussed throughout this book. Harry Triandis, a pioneer in cultural psychology, also conducted cross-national surveys from the 1970s through the present that included a variety of question items such as attitude questions ("Aging parents should live at home with their children—True or False"), rank ordering of lists of value items similar to the Rokeach questionnaire, ratings of scenarios, and if-then sentence completions (If you have money, then you have _____). Triandis has been a major contributor to the analysis of subjective culture as measured by cultural differences along psychological dimensions, especially *individual-collectivism* (Triandis 1990, 1994).

Chapter 2

The Conceptual Framework

The concept of value is linked to the notion of something being good. But what is goodness? Goodness does not seem to be an objective fact since different people find different things good. Goodness appears to be an internal response. Philosophers generally agree that goodness cannot be satisfactorily defined with words—goodness is a prime or primitive term, something we know from direct subjective experience. There are other things like this. Something being funny, or being green in color, or the sense one *should* do something—there are many things that we know about, but cannot define to someone who does not already know about them.

Is goodness just the thought that something is good? Goodness also seems to be a feeling. There is an argument that this affective component is *liking*—if we like something we call it good. This is often true but there it is not clear that substitution of "I like it" for "it is good" results in any conceptual advantage. The term *good* is also used for things that one finds efficient (a good knife), or that do their expected functions well (a good hairdresser). Things one finds beautiful are also normally called *good*. So, liking something, finding something moral or efficient or doing its expected function or being beautiful, are qualities that give rise to the sense of goodness. But that does not make them the same thing as the sense of goodness.

Definitions of Value

The term *value*, like most words, is polysemous. A polysemous word is one that has a number of related senses. For example, the word *man* is polysemous because, depending on context, it can mean a human being (Man versus Dog), a male human (a man versus a woman), an adult male human (a man versus a boy), or a brave adult male human (a man versus a wimp).

The term *value* has at least the following senses.

First, in the phrase "the value of x in this formula," *value* refers to some amount or quantity.

This sense is generally found only in mathematical or linguistic discourse. There is no goodness component in this sense of the term.

Second, value can refer to the preference for something, measured by the preference for that thing over another. Economists use the term *utility* for this sense of value.

In a related vein, Clyde Kluckhohn (1951a) espoused a definition of values as concepts that regulate impulse satisfaction in accordance with the entire array of hierarchical, enduring *goals* of the personality (p. 399). In this formulation values are a selector or choice mechanism that regulates how wants are acted upon as well as the response to external demands.

If one could discover for any person the weights of all the criteria used to choose different courses of action, one would have an incredibly predictive behavioral map, since knowing the criteria that determine choice would allow one to predict everything that person would do. But unfortunately, utility cannot be measured except in very restricted domains of behavior: For example, people prefer more money to less money. Money has utility, and the more of it the better. This single criterion of preferring more money over less money has complex ramifications, but it is a long way from extensive knowledge of *all* of anyone's preferences. It does not predict which people someone will make friends with, or how people will spend their time, or what kinds of things people will buy. Even a relatively simple problem, such as trying to measure the criteria that lead people to buy more Toyotas than Fords, is not easy. Cost, style, colors, frequency of repair, feeling of the ride, steering, safety, view, organization of the controls, dealer friendliness, resale value, satisfaction with one's last car brand, patriotism, and prestige are some of the probable criteria used in car purchases. Finding the weights of these components is very difficult. Car manufacturers would like to know these weights in order to make more attractive cars. But once one begins to investigate the weights for any one of these criteria, the problem arises that most of the criteria mentioned earlier are, in fact, bundles of even more criteria. The criterion of ride feeling, for example, breaks down into many sub-criteria, such as hardness, stiffness, sway, vibration, noise, and so on. To investigate what people prefer just with respect to ride preferences, a large sample of types of rides needs to be produced and then rated by car owners. All this is expensive and time consuming.

In most cases, social scientists do not have direct measures of preference or utility. Rather, they simply observe that people do one thing rather than another (buy more Toyotas than Fords) and then attribute this to some reasonable preference, like low price or good frequency of repair or high resale value. Sometimes social scientists cannot even figure out how to make up a good story about what has been preferred. As has been often noted, once men wore hats, now they do not. For this shift there is no good story about underlying utilities.

The description given earlier concerning the problem of determining preferential criteria is not a caricature. Barth, an ethnographer with extensive experience in investigating people's real-world preferences, found that the more closely one looked, the greater the multivalence of values, distorted by Kluckhohn's phrase that values involved the entire array of hierarchical enduring goals (pp. 34–35). These cautionary words come from someone who has carried out perceptive ethnographic research on cultural preferences. Determining cultural preferences is a grand goal, but probably impossible.

Third, in the phrase "the value of IBM stock has risen 10 percent," *value* refers to price.

Utility and preference are connected to price, but are not the same thing. Water, for example, has great utility for humans. But because the supply of water is normally large, one does not need to pay greatly for it (although this is changing). Price is affected by supply and demand, and so is not intrinsic to the object in the way that utility is. Value as price has a long history of debate in the social sciences, primarily focused on where the price comes from. Early economists, such as Smith, Ricardo, and Marx, thought that the price of objects came from the labor by which they are produced and that is why diamonds have more value than water. The labor theory of value was demolished by Turgot and the economists of the Austrian School who developed the marginal theory of value, although some Marxist-oriented social scientists still use varieties of the labor theory (e.g., Graeber 2001).

Fourth, the default or unmarked meaning of *value* involves a sense of worth—the goodness of something. The term *value* as used here refers to *the goodness attributed to something important*.

Whether something is good or bad appears to be one of the most frequent and salient assessments that humans make. Charles Osgood, a psychologist interested in language and cognition, found that if people rated objects (cats, peaches, thunderstorms) with a broad sample of adjectives (beautiful versus ugly, useful versus not useful, strong versus weak, expensive versus cheap), factor analyses of the adjectives always found that that the first and largest factor was *evaluation*; that is, the good or bad property of things (Osgood et al. 1975). Osgood and his associates carried out this research in over 40 different languages with the same results. (The second factor usually consisted of adjectives involving the strength or power of things, and the third factor the activity or degree of movement of things.) Osgood's findings indicate something we all know; the sense of goodness is a universal response to objects. Indeed, the first thing one usually wants to know about something is—is it good or bad? We humans seem to be wired to respond to things this way. We experience a world that is evaluation saturated.

Sometimes people say that the conscious experience of goodness is the same as preference, because if someone experiences something as good then that person will prefer it over other things experienced as less good. But while it is true that the sense of goodness can affect preferences, many other things affect preference as well, such as habit, addiction, fear of consequences, ideas about social appropriateness, and so on. One often prefers something over something else not because that thing is experienced as better in itself, but because it *leads* to something else that is good. Suppose someone picks the long road home because it goes by a store where needed groceries can be bought. The long road was preferred because of the consequences of taking it, not because the long road, as such, was experienced as good.

However, in the normal sense of the word, values are more than just goodness. Sugar plum fairies are very good, but not things most people value greatly. For something to be a value, it should not only be good, it should also be something that is weighty and important—it should be *worth* something.

Fifth, in phrases such as "He has no values," *values* refer to the moral subset of values.

A person with no moral values is someone who is immoral. Such a person knows that other people feel it is good to help others and bad to steal and cheat, but does not feel this himself. But such a person may have many nonmoral things they feel are good, like money and leisure. This is a specialized or marked sense of the term *value*, referring to a subset of values regarding moral issues.

There are some further semantic problems related to the idea of value. The idea of value can be expressed as a noun, as in "social

Value 1—the amount or quantity of some variable

Value 2—the preference for or utility of something

Value 3—the price of somethng

Value 4—the goodness of something important

Value 5—the degree to which something is morally right

Figure 2.1 Senses of the term *value*.

approval is a universal value." Expressed as a noun, goodness seems to be *in* the thing or event. The idea of value can also be expressed as a verb, as in "he values social approval." As a verb, someone is doing the valuing and the goodness is not in the thing but in the person's *response* to the thing. Although English has both ways of using the idea of value, there seems to be a preference for talking about values as chunks of stuff that have goodness in them, rather than as a response people make to the world. Perhaps it is unsettling to think of goodness as only in us and not at all in the world. Perhaps that is why there are so few common verbs for the internal act of valuing, unlike the large number of terms we have for many other kinds of emotional action, such as the many verbs for love or fear.

This brings us back to a question of whether values are just cognitions or thoughts, or cognitions that include some kind of feeling. As a matter of ordinary talk, people say the experience of goodness is more than just cognition. Obviously, one can know about a value but not hold it. Somebody may know it is considered good to give to charity and even think abstractly that charity is good, yet feel nothing really about charity. The internal sense of its goodness is missing. We speak of a value as *internalized* when a person believes some object or event is good, when the person experiences a strong sense of its goodness and responds with the feelings and motivations that are appropriate to such an appraisal (Spiro 1987). Values vary greatly in the degree they are internalized. Much of the research on values involves trying to measure the degree of internalization.

Research Goals

For this research project, values are defined as the goodness attributed to something important. The expectation is that values will be intercorrelated, forming dimensions or clusters. Organized patterns of values are called *value orientations*. There is a rich vocabulary of terms for different kinds of value orientations; *liberal, conservative, individualistic, collective, communal, interdependent, sociocentric, allocentric, pietistic, evangelical, ascetic, mystic, this worldly, other worldly, traditional, modern, postmodern, libertarian*, and so on. Terms that refer primarily to various institutional spheres of society, such as *capitalistic, socialistic, democratic, authoritarian*, are also often used as shorthand descriptions for the value orientations associated with societies displaying these types of institutions.

Investigation of the organization of values is necessary because there are so many values that it is easy to get lost among the trees. Some structure is needed if the concept is to be used effectively. Social theorists usually develop their own value dimensions; well-known examples are Tönnies's *gemeinschaft* versus *gesellschaft*, Weber's *wertzrationalitat* versus *zweckrationalitat*, and Parsons's *universalism* versus *particularism*. The goal here is to develop a structure of values that corresponds to the actual cognitive structure of people's values. This project began with the hypothesis that values are organized into empirically isolatable clusters and dimensions and that some value dimensions are common to most societies. It was also hypothesized that most societies would display culturally unique value dimensions.

Chapter 3

Questionnaire Construction

Values can be studied by observation, through intensive interviews, by coding cultural representations (advertising, political speeches, newspaper advice columns, etc.), by questionnaire, and through experiments in which people are put in situations in which they are presented with alternatives and asked to select among them, etc. Each method has its own advantages, disadvantages, and advocates. The quantitative research for this project is based on questionnaire data.

There are well-known problems with questionnaires. The same words mean different things to different people. Translations are imperfect. People, however honest their report, do not always respond to the words for things the way they respond to things themselves. Someone may think they value something highly when presented with words—for example, "How much do you value peace and quiet?"— but when presented with lots of peace and quiet, they may find they do not value it as much as they thought. And people may sometimes simply not be able to answer some questions—they just do not know how much they value X, and may never know. Or they may be profoundly ambivalent about something, and both value it and disvalue it, so that no single rating covers the situation.

Despite all these problems, with respect to efficiency and efficacy there is much to be said in favor of questionnaires for the study of values. Observation of the choices someone makes cannot tell us what that person thinks or what he or she feels is good. The most efficient way to find out what people think is to ask them. One can observe people smoking cigarettes but they may or may not think that smoking is a good thing. Experiments can measure preference for those things we are permitted to experiment with, but even that does not tell us how strongly people experience the goodness of something. If we want to know what people experience as good, getting them to tell us is the best method we have until measurement by brain scan improves by several orders of magnitude.

A related advantage to the use of questionnaires is that it is easy to insure that the data is systematically collected; that each person is asked every question. In ethnography and intensive interviewing it is typically impossible to make sure the same questions or observations are made on all individuals. Another advantage of questionnaires is that they are inexpensive to construct and not difficult for people to complete. There may come a time when everything that can be learned about values from questionnaire studies of values has been learned. But at this point in the study of values, questionnaires' data still has a great deal to teach us.

Format

A wide variety of formats have been used in questionnaire construction. Value questionnaires from the 1940s through the 1980s were predominately in the individual question mode. For example:

I would agree to an increase in taxes if the extra money were used to prevent environmental damage.

Such questions can have a number of different kinds of Likert scale format. A typical Likert scale format for this type of question might be as follows:

   1. Strongly Agree   2. Agree   3. Disagree   4. Strongly Disagree

With sentence-based questions, the investigator can pose complex alternatives, qualify choices, and probe for the cognitive schema behind the evaluative judgment. But a major problem with sentences is that it is difficult to know exactly which part of the sentence has affected the respondent's answer. If someone says they strongly agree with the sentence given earlier, is it because they do not mind an increase in taxes, or because they are worried about what has happened to the environment, or because they want to prevent industries from dumping? It could be any of these. Not surprisingly, small changes in wording have strong effects on the ratings of sentences.

These problems have resulted in the development of an alternative, labeled by Kerlinger (1984) as the *multiple referent scale* format. This format uses single words and short phrases, which are then rated on a single-rating scale. Take the following example from the Three Society questionnaire in English (see table 3.1).

Kerlinger found this format to have a number of advantages: It is economical; many items can be administered in a short time, making possible a wide coverage of domains; single words and short phrases tend to be less ambiguous than longer statements; dimensions resulting from principal components or other scaling methods tend to be easy to interpret because there are typically more items per dimension and the

Table 3.1 Kelinger format for Likert scales

		I don't value this	I value this a little	I value this moderately	I value this a lot	I value this very highly
	Circle the number which corresponds to how much you value each item					
85	Government based on laws	0	1	2	3	4
86	Fitting in	0	1	2	3	4
87	Having deep respect for parents	0	1	2	3	4
88	Being practical	0	1	2	3	4

items are relatively simple semantically; the capacity to sample many domains and sub-domains cuts down on experimenter bias in item selection; and the single words and short phrases correspond more directly to people's normal cognitive schemas than more complex sentences (Kerlinger 1984, pp. 120–122). Kerlinger compared the results of the multiple referent format with the standard sentence or statement format for liberalism-conservatism items and found that both formats gave the same general results, with similar correlations between sub-scales.

The advantage of using short phrases when trying to translate from one language to another, plus the greater number of items that can be rated per unit of time, was an important component in the decision to use the multiple reference format. In pretest work, the multiple referents format was found to be more effective than the sentence format, especially with regard to obtaining translation equivalence and making sense of correlations between items.

A format similar to the multiple referents format was developed earlier by Rokeach (1967, 1973). Rokeach used 36 single-word items in his questionnaire (*assertiveness, honest, forgiving, helpful,* etc.) divided equally into two sets of value items that he labeled *instrumental* and *terminal*. Respondents were asked to rank order each set of 18 in terms of their importance to the respondent. Using this technique, in 1968, 1971, 1974, and 1981 representative national samples were interviewed (Rokeach and Ball-Rokeach 1989). Later results from the Rokeach surveys will be compared with the Three Society Project results. The basic drawback of the single-word approach is that many values simply do not have single words to express them. Also it is often the case that single words are more ambiguous and more polysemous than short phrases. In fact, in his questionnaires, Rokeach used a format that had a single term, for example, *salvation,* then in parentheses several other terms—*being saved, eternal life,* and so on, which can have the disadvantage of not clearly stating what is actually being rated.

For this project the most important consideration that worked against the use of rankings is the fact that respondents cannot be expected to rank hundreds of items. While it can be argued that rankings are more precise than ratings, the noisiness of ratings can be offset by increasing sample size. It is an important fact of statistics that imprecise measurements can yield quite precise means given a large sample of unbiased ratings. Also, the correlational analysis of rankings has been found to be more problematic than the correlational analysis of ratings. Correlational analyses of the Rokeach rankings, for example, did not find interpretable component dimensions (Rokeach 1973).

Sampling Items

Sampling values is a major problem. Sampling people can be done quite exactly—each person is assigned a number, and then numbers are randomly selected. But it is impossible to assign each and every value a number because values are not a bounded set; people can value anything they can conceive of. Any topic can be subdivided into finer and finer distinctions; for example, having friends, being with friends, doing things with friends, drinking with friends, talking with friends, reminiscing with old friends, and so on.

One heuristic for locating value items is to select from the values other investigators have studied. For this project a variety of studies were examined, including Florence Kluckhohn (1950), Clyde Kluckhohn (1958), Cora Dubois (1955), Robin Williams (1951), Rokeach (1973), Spindler (1955), Triandis (1994), Fred Kerlinger (1984; see earlier), and Schwartz (1992). At one point the total pool contained over 1,000 potential value items. To help in selecting from this list, a simple classificatory taxonomy was developed. Three research assistants and I selected three hundred and twenty-eight items from this total pool. Items, which were as independent in meaning as possible and as comprehensive of the complete range of semantic meanings as possible, were selected. These three hundred and twenty eight items are presented in appendix A.

Sampling Rating Scales

There is also a sampling problem with respect to selecting *scales* for rating values. Fortunately, the sampling problem is not as great for scales since the number of common evaluative phrases in English is a relatively small set. A limited number of scales are commonly used in value and attitude research; for example, __ is good, I have a positive attitude toward __, __ is important to me, and so on.

Initially, 12 commonly used rating scales were selected. Using these scales a questionnaire was constructed with 20 value items (capitalism, being honest, etc.) and administered to 52 University of California, San Diego (UCSD), undergraduates. Each of the scales was translated into Spanish and Japanese, with standard backtranslation checks. The scale-to-scale correlations were computed across individuals and across value items and z score normalized for each individual. The correlation matrices for each society were submitted to a principal components analysis. The results are presented in table 3.2.

Table 3.2 Principal components analysis of 12 scales across 20 items

	First Component		
	English	*Spanish*	*Japanese*
Is __ important to you?	0.92	0.87	0.92
Does __ mean much to you	0.91	0.88	0.90
Is __ connected to your major goals in life?	0.85	0.83	0.86
Are you motivated by __?	0.87	0.78	0.88
Do you care about __?	0.85	0.81	0.85
How often do you think about __?	0.81	0.75	0.86
Do you have strong feelings about __?	0.73	0.72	0.84
Do you think __ is good?	0.73	0.73	0.75
Do you have a positive attitude about __?	0.73	0.73	0.75
Do your ideas about __ affect how you act?	0.72	0.80	0.66
Do you have many ideas about __?	0.67	0.60	0.70
Are you likely to change what you think about __?	−0.20	0.29	−0.12
Variance accounted for	59%	61%	56%
N	52	46	30

Each scale normalized by individual

Average variance accounted for by the second component = 9%

Items: democracy, capitalism, nuclear energy, drug abuse, ethnic diversity, making money, doing something important, getting an education, competition, following orders, civil rights, helping others, being popular, getting married, self-reliance, being honest, being respected, having fun, going shopping, getting drunk

Format:
1. Is democracy important to you?
Not important |_0_|_1_|_2_|_3_|_4_|_5_|_6_| Very important

In table 3.2 it can be seen that the first component combines both the idea that something is *good* with the idea that it is *important*—that the object is connected to one's major goals, that one cares about it, that it is motivating. This corresponds to the idea of value as defined here—not just the idea that something is good, but also intrinsically linked to affect and motivation, which make the object important.

For all three societies, the first component is very large, with the second component a sixth of the first component, and all following components have eigenvalues less than one. This means that most of what these scales measure is encompassed by a single dimension. When this project was first begun, it was hoped that more than one dimension of evaluation would be found. I had expected that separate evaluative (how good is it), cognitive (how much do you think about it), and motivational (how strongly is the object connected to one's goals) components would be expressed in different components, permitting multiple ratings of the same values. However, what was found was a massive first component, five or six times the size of the second component. Further, the scales with the very highest loadings—how important the object is and how much the object means to you—combine semantically both the idea of the object having a strong evaluative component with a strong affective component.

As a further sampling check, a second questionnaire was constructed with 24 rating scales and 10 value items and administered to 54 UCSD students. The rating scales are given in table 3.3.

It was hoped that by using more scales with a wider range of meanings, including notions of obligation, morality, respect, pride, admiration, and interest, that more than one significant component would emerge. However, the loadings again had the same pattern; a large first component, in this case nine times larger than the second component, with only a small amount of the variance accounted for by the following components.

Given these findings I decided to use just one scale to measure all value items. For the U.S. respondents "How much do you value ___?" was used because it had the highest loading on the first component and because it corresponded most closely with the theoretical term—*value*—which is the object of study. Unfortunately, the American value questionnaire was distributed before trying to translate the Japanese and Vietnamese questionnaire. Surprisingly, no good translation could be found to translate "How much do you value ___?" into either Japanese or Vietnamese. After some experimentation, "How important is ___ to you?" was selected, which Vietnamese and Japanese informants found easy to translate and natural to use.

Table 3.3 Principal components analysis (unrotated) of 24 rating scales across 10 items (54 UCSD students' correlations computed across concepts and respondents)

Scales	Components		
	C 1	C 2	C 3
How much do you value ___	0.95	−0.06	0.01
How important is ___ to you	0.91	0.09	0.00
To what degree is ___ one of your goals	0.91	0.04	0.08
How much do you like ___	0.91	−0.11	0.05
How motivated are you to get ___	0.90	0.02	−0.03
How hard do you try to get ___	0.90	−0.03	−0.07
How good is ___	0.89	−0.24	0.05
To what degree do you have a positive attitude towards ___	0.89	−0.24	0.09
To what degree is ___ one of your interests	0.89	0.12	0.02
To what degree do you have a positive feeling about	0.88	−0.20	0.17
To what degree is ___ a guiding principle in your life	0.86	0.14	0.10
How much does ___ help people	0.85	−0.22	0.02
How much does ___ mean much to you	0.84	0.18	0.07
To what degree are you involved with ___	0.82	0.11	−0.22
How much do you admire others for ___	0.82	−0.22	0.02
Do what degree does ___ make you feel proud	0.81	−0.19	−0.05
To what degree does ___ make you feel respected	0.77	−0.20	−0.06
How often do you think about ___	0.73	0.29	−0.13
To what degree is ___ morally right	0.72	−0.24	0.05
To what degree do you feel obligated to ___	0.70	−0.13	−0.13
How much do you care about ___	0.68	0.46	−0.03
To what degree do you have strong feelings about ___	0.47	0.70	0.03
To what degree do you have many ideas about ___	0.40	0.57	−0.41
How sure are you of your ideas about ___	0.09	0.36	0.86
Variance accounted for	63%	7%	4%

Each scale normalized by individual

Items: competition, having fun, being fair, being friendly, doing a good job, being poor, dieting, cheating, having security, and protecting the environment

As a result of these translation problems, the American English version of the values questionnaire has a different rating scale than the Japanese and Vietnamese versions. To see how much effect this might have, in a separate questionnaire given to 55 UCSD undergraduates 105 items were rated on *value* and *importance* and a correlation of .98 found for the relation between the two for the group means. For all practical purposed the ratings are identical. Based on the strong first component of evaluative rating scales and the close match of the scale "How much do you value ___?" to "How important is ___ to you" with respect to component loadings and correlations across item means, it seems clear that the results would be the same if the questionnaires had all used the *importance* scale.

It is interesting that the term *value* does not seem to have universal currency, and that ratings of *importance* are equivalent to ratings of *value*. Perhaps a term that coveys the fusion of goodness with importance is needed only by social scientists; ordinary people can talk about what is important and assume that goodness goes with importance (why else would it be so important?). Looking at the principal components analyses of rating scales one can see that there are a number of the phrases which have almost identical loadings. Something that means much to one, something that is important, that motivates one, that is connected to major goals, that is good, that one likes, and that one values are apparently so pragmatically similar in the rating context that any of these phrases can be substituted for the others without changing the ratings of the items being judged. The best definition of *value* then, is probably this entire complex of criteria. For me, the center of the semantic complex is the joint operation of motivation and goodness—the formation of an *important good thing.*

Chapter 4

The Three Society Study

In reading the work of Schwartz, and Triandis in the 1990s, I was impressed by the improvements that had occurred in measuring values. It seemed to me that these new methods could be used to answer old questions about the organization of values. Just as in the study of cultural classification systems, techniques of analysis had moved from attempts at feature analysis to the use of multidimensional scaling (Romney 1989); so the study of values had also moved from the intuitive organization of values to the use of multidimensional analysis, especially component analysis, including principal components analysis. I thought that if a very large and varied set of value items could be constructed, ratings of values by respondents from different cultures could be subjected to component analysis, including principal components analysis, and the dimensions of values uncovered. None of the quantitative value studies had used really large numbers of value items. Using 200 or 300 value items, I thought, would make it possible to uncover both universal and culturally specific dimensions for different cultures. Rokeach and Schwartz had not made use of principal components analysis. The result might be the discovery of the kind of dimensions that the Kluckhohns had been searching for.

The Three Society values project was funded by the National Science Foundation from 1997 through 2001. The aim was to develop a large corpus of value items and to administer a values questionnaire to three distinct cultural groups in three different languages. Although it is a small sample, three societies are enough to make it possible to distinguish culturally unique dimensions from potentially universal dimensions. Finding interesting culturally unique dimensions in each of these three cultures would, I thought, make up for the small sample. I knew at the time that Schwartz and others had found a two-dimensional structure with his large sample of societies and 56 value items. Schwartz used a method called *smallest space analysis*, a form of nonmetric multidimensional scaling, rather than component analysis or principal components analysis. Since smallest space analysis is not based on orthogonal metric dimensions Schwartz simply divided up the space into areas based on the way items were clustered in the space. The borders and definitions of the items in these areas evolved over time. After several years of working with cluster labels, Schwartz defined the two basic dimensions of his space as *openness to change* versus *conservation* and *self-enhancement* versus *self-transcendence*. It was my hope that by using a large number of items and standard principal components analysis, among other things, that the Schwartz dimensions could be clarified and more firmly defined.

The three groups selected were Americans (University of California, San Diego [UCSD] undergraduates), Vietnamese refugees in the United States (from the San Diego and Raleigh-Durham areas), and native-born Japanese, primarily living in Japan. The UCSD undergraduates were selected because of the convenience of developing a questionnaire with students who are accessible in settings in which questionnaires can be easily administered. The Vietnamese were selected because April Leininger, then a graduate student in the Department of Anthropology at UCSD, was engaged in field research among the Vietnamese, and she was interested in the way values operate in ordinary life, especially under conditions of culture change. She was separately funded by an NSF predoctoral fellowship. An ethnographic component to the Three Societies project—to give it a name—had not been originally envisaged, but the intellectual advantage of having both questionnaire and field ethnographic observation combined, if only for one of the societies, outweighed considerations of symmetry in research design. Leininger was a collaborator throughout the project, and I am greatly indebted to her for ideas, data, and collegial support.

The Japanese were selected because, although I have never carried out field work in Japan, I have been interested in Japanese culture for years and have worked with a number of Japanese anthropology graduate students and young faculty. After the initial analysis of the Japanese data, Yasusuke Minami at Seijo University became interested in the value project. He kindly checked the translation and administered the questionnaire to a sample of Japanese undergraduates at Seijo University. Minami had carried out field research with tape and video recordings of grade school classrooms, and he consulted with me on the incorporation of some of his published materials into chapter 8. While different in kind from Leininger's Vietnamese ethnographic data, the inclusion of Minami's ethnographic data made possible a comparison of primary materials concerning institutional values to personal values.

The Second Puzzle

Chapters 3 and 4 describe the methods used to develop and analyze the Three Society questionnaire. There were some unanticipated problems in developing the questionnaire, which finally contained 328 items translated into Japanese and Vietnamese. However, the major problem that emerged was simply the results. In chapters 4 and 5 these results are presented at length. Suffice it to say here that (1) only three dimensions were discovered; (2) no culturally unique dimensions were discovered; (3) the differences between the Americans, the Vietnamese, and the Japanese were very much smaller than expected.

The most dissonant finding was the small size of the differences between societies. Using Cohen's *d* (1988) as a measure of the size of effect, the average difference between societies is approximately 0.34 of a standard deviation (computed from *d* scores for all pairs of societies for all 328 items). Although small, a third of standard deviation difference will be statistically significant with samples of 60 or more. In fact, the 70 percent of the 984 value item comparisons for the Three Society study are statistically significant; we can be *reasonably* sure that there are real value differences between the three societies. But, while real, these differences are not impressive.

The small size of the *average* difference for the 984 comparisons might have been composed of many very small differences and a few large differences. But this was not the case; only 45 of the 984 comparisons showed a mean difference of greater than one standard deviation, not quite 5 percent. Only one comparison showed a difference of two standard deviations: the Vietnamese rate *having a well-ordered society* much more highly than the Japanese do.

By 1999 the high degree of similarity in values between the three groups had become glaringly apparent in the Three Societies data. In 2001, Schwartz and Bardi published a paper that demonstrated this same high level of similarity among societies for a large sample of 56 national groups. In a sense this was reassuring because it indicated that the results of the American, Vietnamese, and Japanese value study were not due to some statistical artifact. Yet in another sense it made things worse, since these results further contravened so much ethnographic work accomplished by so many ethnographers over so many decades. Schwartz and Bardi did not discuss the discrepancy between their findings with the usual expectation of large value differences between societies, but they do admit to some surprise: "We discovered that, along with striking differences, there is a surprising degree of consensus across individuals and groups that certain values are especially important (e.g., honesty and other proso-cial values) and that others are much less important (e.g., wealth and other power values)" (Schwartz and Bardi 2001, p. 268). To date there has been little speculation or discussion in the literature about the surprisingly small size of cultural differences in values.

As a result of the failure to find large cultural differences, the Three Society project changed its direction toward trying to understand this phenomenon. The first attempt focused on a search for less obvious kinds of statistical differences. There were some successes in this ven-ture, which are presented in the chapters that follow. However, in was in working with Leininger's and Minami's ethnographic data, as well as with published ethnographic reports by Fujita, Sano, Shimizu, and others about Japanese norms and values, that ideas first began to emerge that could explain the apparent paradox.

These ideas are presented in the later chapters of this book. While this is not the place to present these explanations in detail, suffice it to say that there are two aspects of values that differ greatly by society, and even by institution and group. The first involves "what-counts-as-what." To take a simple example, for some people the right to choose with respect to abortion counts as a woman's right to privacy and self-determination, while for others abortion is not a true right at all, but instead counts as a way by which some women immorally evade their responsibilities. Both sides agree on the value of being responsible, and on the values of privacy and self-determination. What is different is how these values are *linked* to the world. It seems to those who make the connection one way that it is perfectly natural to see the world their way, and they find it aggravating that what-counts-as-what for them does not count the same way for others. To them, the others seem perverse, and to have different values. But the difference is not a difference in values per se, but in what counts as expressing or embodying or exemplifying these values. The point made in this book is that when one encounters a society where people do not hook their values to norms and practices the way one does one-self, one is likely to think that what is different about the culture of these people is that it has *different values*. In classroom discussions, for example, I have found that right-to-life advocates will sometimes refuse to believe that the choice advocates could possibly value life as much as they do. This explanation says that the finding of small differences between societies in the value data could be correct because what makes for the large differences between societies is what-counts-as-what, not in what is valued. Ethnographers and casual observers see that people have different norms and cultural practices, and they then attribute the values *they* would have to have if they were to do the things they observe people to be doing. This is a fundamental error in attribution.

A second, quite different explanation for the small value differences between societies was developed toward the end of this project. This explanation grew from an initial finding that the values endorsed by the Americans were quite different and that the values that these same Americans believed were *typical* of Americans, as discussed in the chapter on American values. This result suggested that people might live in shared value worlds that were not the same as the world of the actual personal values held by individuals. It was a simple matter to make another values questionnaire and ask respondents "What are the values that are important to __?" where __ could be any role, like that of being a *mother*, or a *teacher*, or a *governor*. Obviously, many of the values that are important to being a *mother* are quite different from the values that are important to being a *business entrepreneur*. Once it became obvious that *personal* values were not the same as the values ascribed to roles, one could then ask whether the values of Japanese *social institutions*, for example, were systematically different than the *personal* values of the Japanese people. The later section of this book takes up this idea and argues that the conflict between personal values and institutional values is a part of life and creates conflicts and problems for both society and the individual.

Finally, toward the end of the book, a conflict theory concerning the generation of values is presented, which argues that value standards are formulated by individuals and cultures when there is a certain type of conflict. This type of conflict is one in which A is in some kind of opposition to B, but one cannot do without a certain amount of A as well as a certain amount of B. Some informal cross-cultural evidence for this theory is presented. Thus, in chapter 10, the contrast noted by Barth (1993) between the Baktaman, who are generous but do not have strong generosity values, and the Balinese, who are quite acquisitive but do have strong generosity values, is used as an illustration of the hypothesis that doing good things without conflict does not lead to the formation of cultural values, while doing good things with conflict is likely to lead to the formation of cultural values.

If this book does what is intended, then when the reader finishes the last chapter, some of the mistaken conceptualizations that led to the apparent paradox that different societies are both similar and yet very different in values will be obvious. However, more than just therapeutic shedding of bad ideas, a further purpose of this book is to add to understandings about how values actually work on both the personal and social level. Values are an important part of human life, but the way they operate is more complicated than current formulations indicate. This is a rich and as yet relatively uncharted area for investigation.

Chapter 5

The Organization of Values

This chapter describes the organization of value items into a taxonomy of clusters and dimensions. The approach used here makes no assumptions about the content of the categories or dimensions that may be found. The basic assumption is that ratings of items with similar meanings will be more highly correlated across individuals than items with unrelated meanings and from that all else follows.

Method Problems

The value questionnaire was administered to 210 UCSD undergraduates, 248 Vietnamese living in the United States, and 61 native-born Japanese, of which over half were resident in the Japan. A second sample of 201 Japanese undergraduates collected by Yasusuke Minami is also discussed later. The sampling procedures and demographics for each sample are presented in more detail in the chapters on American, Vietnamese, and Japanese values.

The first step of the analysis was to carry out cluster analysis and principal components analyses of the item-to-item value correlations (Pearson r). Principal components and component analysis are very similar methods, differing only in the treatment of communalities—the diagonal elements placed in the correlation matrix that determine whether only the shared variance (component analysis) or the total observed variance will be analyzed. It is generally agreed that the differences produced by the two methods are small, and "will virtually disappear when the number of variables per component is large" (Goldberg and Digman 1994, p. 222). Principal components analysis has been used throughout in the study because, unlike component analysis, it does not need to assume that the dimensions found in the analysis correspond directly latent to real-world entities.

However, before undertaking a cluster or principal components analysis, a decision had to be made with respect to normalizing the data. A number of components, such as social desirability, can affect individual ratings. There are also other kinds of individual differences; for example, some people tend to use the whole range of a scale for their ratings while others tend to use just a segment of the scale. This affects the correlations between items because if some people use only the high end of the scales and some use only the low end, the correlations between items will be inflated. This is a common problem with rating scales, and one of the reasons that some researchers on values prefer to use rankings rather than ratings.

Ipsatization

One technique for reducing the effects of differences in how individuals use scales is to *ipsatize* the data. The term *ipsatization* is a stranger to most dictionaries. Ipsatization—making things the same—involves normalizing scores so that every individual has the same mean and the same standard deviation across all items. This does not affect relationships between items—an individual's high items are still equally high for that individual and the low items are equally low—but it puts every individual on an identical scale. One standard way to ipsatize is to compute z scores so that the mean across items for each individual is adjusted to zero and the standard deviation to one. This, in effect, turns the raw score ratings into calibrated rankings.

While ipsatization takes care of the problem that different individuals may use different ranges of the scale, it creates other problems. Ipsatizing data creates stronger negative correlations than would be found with the unstandardized data. The expected decrease in the correlation coefficients is $1/(n-1)$, where n is the number of items (Dunlap and Cornwell 1994). For large samples, the effect is not great. For the Three Society data, ipsatization results in a decrease of 0.12 in the mean correlation between items. However, ipsatization can remove the first component that is present in unipsatized data. If the first component is not wanted because it is only a measure of social desirability or the like, then loss of the first component is a good thing. If it has important information, it is a bad thing.

The literature on the pros and cons of ipsatization is large and complex (Baron 1996, Bertam 1996, Dunlap and Cornwell 1994, Cattell and Brennan 1994, Rankin and Grube 1980). For the various structural analyses of the data reported here, the analyses were carried out on both ipsatized and unipsatized data sets. Both kinds of analyses yield similar components and clusters, although the ipsatized data revealed clearer and more interpretable results. If not further specified, reported results are for ipsatized data. One strong reason to ipsatize cross-cultural data presented by Oishi et al. (1998) is that some societies tend to show display response sets in which all value items are given high ratings. Ipsatization removes this effect. Goldberg and Digman (1994) recommend that when more than 100 items are involved, each individual's responses be separately standardized into z scores across the total set of items, "thereby attenuating the problems caused by individual differences in subjects' response distributions" (p. 219).

Reliability

One of the most important things to know about ratings is whether or not they are *reliable*. Given items rated on a five-point Likert scale, one cannot help wondering whether the marks one sees on the paper questionnaires reflect something real. The degree of reliability displayed by a scale answers this question. If a scale, with repeated applications, gives the same measurements, the scale is reliable, and if a scale is reliable logic says it must be measuring *something*, because only if it were measuring *something* could it produce the same results more than once. What it measures may not be what one thinks it measures (the issue of exactly *what* is being measured is a question of *validity*).

For questionnaire data, there are different ways to measure reliability. The most direct of these is to give the same questionnaire to the same persons more than once—test-retest reliability, as it is called. To obtain test-retest data, the 328-items questionnaire was given to 25 UCSD undergraduates and then retested on them six weeks later. The mean correlation between the first and second test, using individuals as the unit of analysis and averaging across items, was 0.53. These figures are consistent with the test-retest reliability correlation of 0.48 that Rankin and Grube found for a sample of 236 undergraduates using five-point ratings of the 36 Rokeach value items (Rankin and Grube 1980).

A test-retest correlation of 0.53 for individuals is not high. However, individually based test-retest reliability figures greatly underestimate the reliability of *group means* when there is group consensus about the items being measured. One way to demonstrate this is to randomly divide the sample for one of the societies into two groups of respondents and then correlate the means of the two groups with each other. For the American sample, the first random division of the sample into two groups resulted in a correlation of 0.97 between the means for the 328 items. Thus, the two randomly divided halves of the sample agreed almost perfectly with each other. Value items that had high means in one group also had high means in the other group. This is a good measure or reliability. Of course, a different random split would yield a different correlation. Fortunately, it is possible to calculate the average correlation for *all* possible split halves using a coefficient called Cronbach's *alpha*. While alpha is usually used to measure the reliability of multi-item *scales*, using alpha to measure the reliabilities of group *means* given normalized data is mathematically sound (Guilford 1936). The alphas for the American, Japanese, and Vietnamese samples were all above 0.98. These high alphas show that the ratings are reliable measures of the sample means.

High group alphas are typically the result of strong group consensus. Consensus—agreement in belief by the members of a group—has been a major focus of anthropological research since the pioneering work of Romney, Weller, and Batchelder in the 1980s (Romney et al. 1986). Impressive cultural consensus has been found in a wide variety of domains, including color terms, properties of illnesses, word associations, plant terms, job titles, models of family relationships, and lifestyles (Boster 1987). A more complete investigation of the degree of consensus within each society is presented in chapter 6.

Correlations between Value Items and the Construction of Scales

Unlike the correlations between individuals, the correlations between value items for the three samples are relatively low, with a mean absolute correlation for the three matrices (minus the diagonals) of 0.095. It is likely that the low reliability of the Likert rating scales has affected the correlations, as well as the effects of ipsatization. It may seem paradoxical that the value data can display good reliability with respect to *group* means but low reliability for correlations. This happens because, for group means, random error or noise cancels out across the judgments of many respondents. But, in the computation of a correlation, random error does not cancel out across respondents. Rather than being canceled, error or noise becomes a constant that decreases or attenuates the correlation coefficient; the greater the error variance, the less the amount of variance that can be accounted for by the relationship between the variables. Noisy data results in low correlations. However, the relative strength of correlations—that variable A is more strongly correlated with variable B than it is with variable C—should not be affected by random noise. So while we do not know with much certainty exactly how strongly A is correlated with B, we can know with considerable certainty that A is more strongly correlated with B than with C.

The 58 Clusters of Value Items

Our first step in working out the organization of value items was to construct clusters of correlated items using the joint correlation matrix for all three societies. Both cluster analysis and principal components analysis were used to construct clusters. The technique of cluster analysis used here was the standard average link method that begins by putting the most highly correlated single items together into small clusters, and then adding to these clusters on the basis of the highest average correlation between clusters (Aldenderfer and Blashfield 1984).

Overall, the process of scale construction is an iterative one. One begins by first putting together groups of items that are generally intercorrelated, then eliminating those items that have less consistent correlations with other items in the cluster, then searching for better items that might be placed within this cluster, and repeating the process until one cannot improve the clusters one has (Comrey and Lee 1992). The overall goal is to construct clusters with the highest average correlation between items and lowest correlation between clusters. Following this procedure, 58 clusters were constructed from the 328 value items. Numerous trade-offs were involved in the process. Sometimes, based on the correlations, an item could equally well be placed in more than one cluster; so the deciding factor tended to be the semantic clarity of the resulting cluster. Sometimes a cluster could be broken up and its items reallocated with some loss in the clarity of cluster structures but an offsetting increase in reliability because the clusters were then all larger. Although the subjective element in constructing clusters may make the process seem unscientific, what counts in the end is the *effectiveness* of the constructed clusters—how well these clusters account for the total data and how reliable they are. These characteristics can be assessed quite objectively.

One direct measure of the effectiveness of a clustering procedure is to ask how much of the total variance is accounted for by the clusters. This is a straightforward analysis of variance problem with 58 categories and 328 scores (each score is the mean across individuals for that value item). For all three samples, over 60 percent of the total variance is accounted for by the 58 cluster categories. This is quite a substantial amount—the data has been reduced from 328 numbers to 58 numbers for each respondent yet retains 60 percent of all the information contained in the 328 numbers. Furthermore, it is likely that much of the variance that has been lost is random noise, since the common variance tends to be contained in the averages of the items that make up the scales.

Another objective measure of the effectiveness of multi-item clusters is the reliability of the clusters as scales. Alphas can be calculated for multi-item scales using the mean correlation between the items where n is the number of items that make up the scale (Cronbach 1951). As described earlier, an alpha of 0.70 indicates that if one divided the items of the cluster in half, the correlation between the two halves, averaged across all possible ways of splitting the items, would be 0.70. Unfortunately, alphas for item clusters are often misused as a criterion for assessing the value of group results. Even in excellent meta-reviews, such as the Oyserman et al. review discussed later, strong criticism tends to be made of studies where internal cluster alphas are less than 0.70. Such criticism is not warranted if the investigator is generalizing across *group* means rather than *individual* scores. Thus Oyserman et al. were surprised that the studies with low internal cluster alphas sometimes found group differences that were larger than studies with high internal cluster alphas. Generally, low reliability results in more noise and weaker results, so how could less reliable scales yield stronger results? But this is not surprising once one realizes that a group mean can be just as reliable for a scale with a low alpha as for a scale with high alpha if there is strong group consensus. For example, the internal alphas for the 58 clusters had an average of 0.52 but the group mean alphas for the 58 clusters averaged above 0.98 for the three societies.

Overall, the 58 clusters are conceptually clear and well bounded. Items tend to be organized around concrete topics, such as *family* or *being a good person*, rather than around more abstract concepts, such as *mastery* or *hierarchy*. Interpretation of the meaning of a cluster is based on the specific items that make up cluster. Clusters can serve as an important check on translation problems, since single phrases are more easily mistranslated than whole clusters of phrases. The appendix, at the end of this book, which contains all the items for each cluster, shows in the bar graphs for each cluster the degree to which the items that make up a cluster have similar mean ratings. In fact, most of the cluster items have similar ratings, indicating the high likelihood that they share a core of common meaning.

All this information about scales, components, reliability, social desirability, ipsativity, and the like may be more than the average reader wants to know. It is temping to leave this material out and ask the reader to just assume that things were done properly. But at this point in time with respect to the cross-national analysis of values the statistical problems discussed earlier have not been settled, and almost any choice is controversial. The different choices affect the results and can give rise to the kind of difficulties described later with respect to the meta-analysis of individualism and collectivism by Oyserman et al. (2002).

The Top Taxonomic Level

The 58 clusters represent the first level of organization above the specific items. To investigate the organization of the data at a more abstract level, a principal components analysis was carried out on a correlation matrix based on the data from 60 American, 60 Japanese, and 60 Vietnamese respondents. The data from each society was standardized by individual and by value item, insuring that correlations between items are not increased by societal differences in value profiles. Leung and Bond (1998) call this operation "deculturing" the data. To check, a second principal components analysis was carried out on undercultured data. The results of the two analyses were highly similar. A third analysis based on the average correlations of the American, Japanese, and Vietnamese correlation matrices was also carried out, which again show highly similar results. The point of all these checks is to insure that the results are not an artifact of cultural differences in response acquiescence or some other response characteristic.

The principal components analysis, presented in table 5.1, displays a structure of three independent and interpretable dimensions. Not presented here because of space limitations, a principal components analysis of the full 328 individual items (for the entire sample, including the Japanese college students) yielded the same three dimensions. Attempts to find more dimensions that were robust and stable were unsuccessful. Small shifts in the number of items or clusters being analyzed resulted in large shifts in component loadings after the first three dimensions.

The same three dimensions were also found in the principal components analyses for each of the societies analyzed separately. The three dimensions when rotated into conformity with each other have a mean correlation of 0.80. The first two dimensions form reliable scales for individual assessment. The first dimension, *individualism* versus *collectivism*, has an alpha of 0.83, *altrusim* versus *self-interest* has an alpha of 0.80, and *industriousness* versus *relaxation* has an

Table 5.1 Principal components analysis of 58 value clusters (*combined matrix for Americans, Japanese, and Vietnamese. Coefficients are factor loadings for the 3 components. Individual items for each cluster can be found in Appendix A*)

Individualism versus Collectivism

Individualism	Collectivism
Personal exploration	*Societal obligations*
0.6 Being open to change	−0.6 Defending my country
0.6 Being creative	−0.5 The US military, the death sentence, National Security
0.6 Living a life of adventure	
0.2 Understanding science	−0.4 Being religious
0.4 Liking art and literature	−0.3 Having law and social order
0.3 Resisting authority	
	Personal obligations
Self-expression	−0.4 Being sexual restrained
0.5 Sexual freedom	−0.5 Being respectful and polite
0.4 Being relaxed and enjoying life	−0.5 Working for the group and doing what others expect of me
0.4 Having fun	
0.3 Having love and a satisfying sexual life	
	−0.6 Maintaining tradition
0.3 Having time alone	−0.6 Having a close-knit family
Self-determination	*Circumspection*
0.4 Feeling sure about myself	−0.4 Being careful
0.4 Choosing my own goals	−0.3 Being thrifty
0.3 Being optimistic	
0.3 Self-fulfillment	

Alruism versus Self-interest

Altruism	Self-interest
Egalitarianism	*Success*
0.6 Treating people equally	−0.7 Having nice things, good looks, taste, success, etc.
0.6 Respecting others feelings	
0.4 Finding meaning in life	−0.7 Having social status
0.3 Being honest and genuine	−0.5 Being prosperous
0.2 Having close friends	
	Self-advancement
Social amelioration	−0.5 Being ambitious and competitive
0.6 Working for social improvement	
	−0.3 Keeping fit
0.5 Living in harmony with nature	−0.2 Market competition, economic growth, capitalism
0.4 Public schools, the UN, health care	
0.4 Avoiding war	*Acceptance*
	−0.4 Being liked and belonging
Personal adjustment	
0.3 Being able to adust	
0.2 Controlling myself	

Continued

Table 5.1   Continued

Industry versus Relaxation	
Industry	*Relaxation*
Striving	*Amusements*
0.6 Having high standards	−0.4 Sleeping, eating, drinking
0.3 Pursuing knowledge and being	alcohol
well informed	−0.3 Watching movies, tv,
0.3 Being a leader	eating out
	−0.3 Enjoying comics, board
Diligence	games, sports
0.6 Being persistent	
0.6 Working hard	*Disengagements*
0.5 Being orderly and regular	−0.2 Being detached and
0.4 Being responsible	accepting one's fate
	−0.3 Believing in omens,
Canniness	mysticism, dreams, luck,
0.3 Planning for the future	psychics
0.2 Being practical and realistic	

alpha of 0.66. These figures indicate that *individualism* versus *collectivism* and *altruism* versus *self-interest* can be measured quite reliably at the individual level as well as at the group level, but that *self-interest* versus *industriousness* is somewhat less reliable as a measure on the individual level.

While only three dimensions were found, it is likely that more than three cross-culturally valid value dimensions exist. However, the dimensions yet to be discovered may not be orthogonal to the dimensions already discovered, or may tend to fuse with the universal components. If a more reliable method of obtaining value ratings could be developed, it is possible and even likely that a variety of culturally unique components would be discovered.

A Second Taxonomic Level

The 58 clusters form the first level of organization, one that is relatively close to the data, grouping items together by common topics. The principal components analysis of the clusters, on the other hand, tells us about the top level of organization; the most general and abstract features that saliently apply to these topics. Between the two, it is possible to distinguish a middle level of organization; one that places together the 58 clusters into higher-level clusters. An average-link cluster analysis of the 58 clusters produced 17 macro clusters. These mid-level clusters are helpful in understanding and presenting the organization of values, although they are not as unitary in their composition as the 58 clusters. The taxonomy for the three dimensions, 17 macro clusters, 58 clusters, and 328 items is presented in the appendix, along with the means and bar graphs for each society, the effect sizes of the differences between the means, and the significance level of these differences.

The First Dimension: *Individualism* versus *Collectivism*

The top-level first component for the combined Three Society data, presented in table 5.1, is the *individualism* versus *collectivism* dimension (Hofstede 1980, Triandis 1994). In table 5.1 each of the 58 clusters is placed on the component on which it had its highest loading, given immediately to the right of each cluster label. A more complete four-level taxonomy, which includes the individual items, is found in the appendix. Given the hope of finding culturally unique dimensions, it was disconcerting to find the well-studied *individualism* versus *collectivism* dimension emerging as the first component in the analyses, not only in the combined correlation matrix analysis, but in each of the separate analyses for Americans, Japanese, and Vietnamese. Using a large variety of items did not attenuate or obscure the clear importance of this dimension.

An extensive meta-analysis of cross-society research on individualism and collectivism has been published by Daphna Oyserman, Heather Coon, and Markus Kemmelmeier (2002). The Oyserman et al. review, after examining a large number of different *individualism* and *collectivism* scales, presents a summary of the most general and common defining qualities of these dimensions. In addition to value items, Oyserman et al. include psychological traits, such as reasoning styles, emotional regulation, and worldview assumptions in their descriptions. Oyserman et al. describe *individualism* as a positive sense of an independent self, along with a high evaluation of feeling good about oneself, being emotionally open, having personal success, and having many unique and distinctive personal qualities.

For the Three Society data, *individualism* as a value orientation is based on values concerning personal exploration, expressing oneself, and determining ones own goals. More salient in the Three Society data than in the Oyserman et al. definition of *individualism* is the expression of selfhood in pleasures—having fun, relaxing, having love and sex, and so on. There is also an emphasis on adventure, privacy, and being different. The picture that emerges is a kind of romantic celebration of the self—what one might imagine a wonderful undergraduate life would be like. This dimension of individualism does not involve arrogating oneself over others, or being selfish.

Ingelhart (1997) has pointed out that individualism tends to increase as societies move from more traditional or industrial social systems to the postindustrial, service-, market-, and media-oriented societies of the advanced economies. This complex of features has also been found to strongly correlate cross-nationally with ratings of life satisfaction and well-being (Diener et al. 1995). In these studies respondents are asked to rate how satisfied they are with their life. The means for societies are then compared and correlated with other societal characteristics. Diener et al. find that national ratings of subjective well-being are correlated with national wealth (GDP per capita), strong human rights, equality of income, and *individualism* as measured by Triandis and Hofstede. It is not surprising that countries that are richer, less unequal, and where people enjoy good legal and social rights would have more satisfying lives, and thereby rate themselves as happier and more satisfied. More surprising is the finding that *individualism* is more highly correlated with subjective well-being than any other of these other predictors, and that even controlling for wealth, equality, and rights, individualism remains strongly related to subjective well-being. However, there is some dispute about this (Arrindell et al. 1997).

Individualism as a value orientation is also conceptually and empirically related to a major personality dimension, called *openness*, which has emerged from studies of the Big Five personality dimensions (Roccas et al. in press). Major facets of *openness* include being imaginative, having artistic interests and concern with intellect, being open in emotional expression, and adventurousness. Further discussion of the relation between value orientations and personality components are presented later with reference to the Vietnamese data.

The clusters for *collectivism* form the opposite side of this dimension. *Collectivism*, Oyserman et al. found, is typically based on items concerning the placement of a high value to ties to others and to the groups and institutions that create these ties. *Collectivism* scales also typically contain items concerning those personal qualities that assist in attaining group goals, such as sacrifice for the common good, maintaining harmonious relations with close others, and restraint in emotional expression (Oyserman et al., pp. 9–11, 18–20).

For the Three Society data, *collectivism* centers on the positive evaluation of the enduring institutions and groups that make up society. It should be pointed out that the elements that make up *collectivism* are not just groups of people. Tradition and law, for example, refer to institutions, not social groups. The groups that are included with *collectivism* are notable sources of social solidarity in modern society—family, religion, and nation—, which are sometimes referred to as the basic sources of diffuse primordial sentiments of solidarity. It is striking that the institutions of the market and the groups formed by companies are excluded from this dimension. *Individualism* values the singular *I*, *collectivism* the plural *We*. Perhaps the business world seems more on the side of the singular *I* than the plural *We*.

It is significant that this dimension as an entity lacks a good single term to refer to it. Perhaps this is because one cannot define *collectivism* as *not individualism* (as *not* valuing *openness*, or *not* valuing *freedom*, or *not* valuing *self-determination*, etc.). Nor can one define *individualism* as *not collectivism* (as *not* valuing *family*, *religion*, *nation*, *tradition*, etc.). Oyserman et al., in their review, treat the poles separately, since they find that things that correlate positively with one pole do not always correlate negatively with the other pole. Here, however, the principal components analysis of the Three Society data definitely places *individualism* and *collectivism* on opposite sides of the same component. This issue is discussed further later.

Altruism versus *Self-Interest*

The second dimension of the cluster principal components analysis is labeled *altruism* versus *self-interest*. As a bipolar construct, this dimension corresponds to Schwartz's dimension of *Self-Transcendence* versus *Self-Enhancement* on the societal level (which he terms *Harmony* and *Egalitarianism* versus *Hierarchy* and *Mastery* on the individual level) (Sagiv and Schwartz 2000). *Altruism* items center on egalitarianism, helping people, and being tolerant and empathetic. Moderately strong loadings are found for avoiding war, supporting health care, unions, schools, and environmentalism. Finding meaning in life, begin honest, being able to adjust, control oneself, and having friendships also show moderate loadings.

Schwartz and his associates found *Self-Transcendence* to be closely related to one of the Big Five personality components called *agreeableness*, marked by character traits such as warmth, friendliness, and helpfulness (McCrae and Allik 2002, Roccas et al. 2002). Both the personality component and the value orientation focus on other *people* as their primary referent. What is different about the personality dimension is that it has a clear contradictory pole, characterized by traits such as being cold, hostile, and mean. In contrast, the other end of the *altruism* pole is not characterized by treating others badly. Instead, the other pole refers to having good things, getting ahead, being a success, and so on. The basic value contrast is *good-to-other* versus *good-to-self*, while the basic contrast for the personality dimension is *good-to-other* versus *bad-to-other*. One reverses the object, the other reverses the action.

The *self-interest* pole includes hierarchical, competitive, self-arrogating items, as well as nonhierarchical items involving *being employed, being healthy, being liked, fitting in*, and so on. This point is important, because it is tempting to treat the difference between *altruism* versus *self-interest* as nothing more than a contrast between egalitarianism versus hierarchy. But, in the Three Society data, hierarchy is a secondary feature of the *self-interest* dimension; the primary emphasis is on taking care of oneself.

A scatter plot for the combined loadings for 44 value clusters that have their highest loadings on these two dimensions is presented in figure 5.1.

The clusters on the graph form a rough circumplex—a circle of points around two dimensions. The clusters *treating people equally, working for social justice*, and *respecting others' feelings*, found at 12 o'clock, are the highest loading items for *altruism*. Moving clockwise around the circumplex to 2 o'clock, the clusters *being able to adjust* and *liking art and literature* have loadings on both *altruism* and *individualism*. At 3 o'clock there is a dense grouping of clusters that define the *individualism* pole, such as *being open to change, being creative*, and *enjoying life*. The cluster for *being ambitious and competitive* is found at 4:30, combining both *individualism* and *self-interest*. At 6 o'clock two clusters are found, which include a large number of items such as owing a good stereo, a nice car, a house, being well dressed, having good looks, having good taste, being a success, having social status, and being famous. These seem to express *self-interest* in pure form. Closely related is the *being prosperous* cluster. There are not many clusters that combine *self-interest* and *collectivism*; the most salient is the *being liked and belonging* cluster, which includes specific items as *being approved of, having others think well of me, feeling that one belongs, fitting in*, and *having a good reputation*. At 9 o'clock in the graph there is a dense grouping of classic collectivist items; *family, religion, sexual restraint, tradition*, the *military*, and so on. Finally, rounding the circumplex and moving toward 11 o'clock where both *collectivism* and *altruism* are

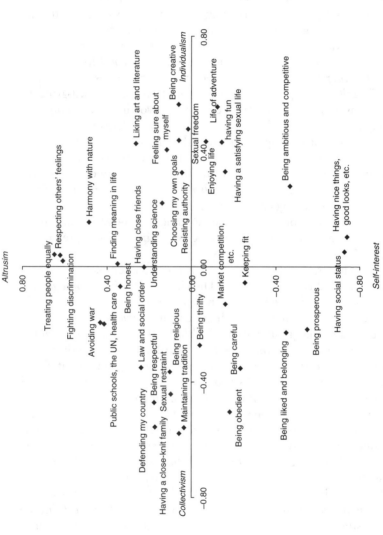

Figure 5.1 Principal components analysis of 58 values clusters: combined American, Japanese and Vietnamese data.

salient, one finds *law and social order,* then *avoiding war* and a cluster that includes *public schools, the UN, national health care, labor unions,* and *democracy.*

Related Research on the Circumplex Structure of Values

Other cross-society studies have found the same circumplex. Schwartz, beginning with the items used by Rokeach, developed a list of over 50 value items, which were administered to a large number of societies. Figure 5.2 presents the smallest space analysis for 56 value items adapted from Schwartz (1992). Correlations were computed across the means of the 80 samples and submitted to a smallest space analysis (Borg and Lingoes 1987). All in all, figure 5.2 summarizes a great amount of data, collected from all over the world, representing the most extensive cross-national research on values in the literature. Dimensional labels of *individualism* versus *collectivism* and *altruism* versus *self-interest* have been added to the graph in italics. Overall, there is a remarkable fit between the Schwartz's data and the Three Society data. The hypotheses of two universal value dimensions, labeled here *altruism* versus *self-interest* and *collectivism* versus *individualism*, has strong empirical support.

A somewhat different circumplex has been described by Inglehart (1997). Inglehart's 42 items include values and beliefs, as well as attitudes. In a principal components analysis he finds two dimensions labeled as *well-being* versus *survival* and *secular-rational authority* versus *traditional authority.* The items that define *traditional authority* match the *collectivism* items (national pride, obedience, religious faith, and family). However, for Inglehart the opposite side of this cluster is not the same as the *individualism* pole. Instead, his *secular-rational authority* pole includes items relating to determination, thrift, and an interest in politics, as well as individualist items such as approval of abortion and divorce. His *well-being* pole contains a number of items whose content matches the *individualism* pole (imagination, tolerance, choice, and leisure) but the opposing pole, *survival,* contains items whose content involves a broad mixture of the Three Society dimensions (state responsibility, unhappiness, hard work, rejection of outgroups, money, etc.). It is likely that the difference between Inglehart's and the Three Society dimensions is due to the fact that Inglehart includes both beliefs and specific attitude items in

Figure 5.2 Recomputed smallest space analysis 70 cultural groups (recomputed from Schwartz [2002]).

his analysis. Many of the clusters of items are similar in the two analyses, but the positions of these clusters are slightly different.

Why? The Individual versus Society

In looking at the composition of these three dimensions, one cannot help but be impressed with the degree to which the organization of the items is centered on the relation of the individual to society. The starkest contrast is between altruism and self-interest. Both are necessary in human life. As a social species, we survive only if we support each other. As individual organisms, however, we survive only if we take care of ourselves. Similarly, we need to have both the social solidarity that comes with joining and having obligations to groups to become individuals. Even the third dimension, with its contrast between work and relaxation, indirectly involves the tension between the social world and the self. One can carry these speculations further and consider the evolutionary forces that help form the basic capacity for human value orientations. The human psyche experiences things more complex than pleasure—we experience goodness, and with it the sense that we should be good. Altruistic, collectivistic, and industrious values not only have the capacity to motivate human action, but they also serve to justify attacks on those who are too self-interested, too individualistic, and not hard working enough. This may be one of the most important functions that values have— they not only influence choice, they *legitimate* actions and they *legitimate* punitive sanctions on failures to act correctly. There is an interesting literature in the human evolution field that worries about how the in-built motivations to sanction social defectors could have developed given the fact that there is likely to be a cost to the individuals who do the sanctioning. This involves the problem of a second-order defection—people who might want to punish defectors look at the cost in terms of their own self-interest and also defect by not risking carrying out the punishment. The sharing of values spreads the risk in attacking defectors across many individuals—not just those directly hurt—and offers strong secondary rewards of esteem and approval to those who are actively on patrol.

Despite the convergence of findings concerning the general character of the value circumplex formed by the intersection of *individualism* versus *collectivism* and *altruism* versus *self-interest*, there are some doubts that these dimensions are really bipolar. Schimmack, Oishi, and Diener (2004) argue that it is likely that individualism and collectivism are really two single-pole dimensions, a position also taken by Oyserman et al. (2002). Schimmack et al. note that the ipsatization carried out by Hofstede, Triandis, and others, which they agree is needed to control for acquiescence and over endorsement effects, can give rise to a statistical artifact in which bipolar dimensions are created by the increase in negative correlations resulting from ipsatization.

If *individualism* versus *collectivism* and altruism versus *self-interest* are not really bipolar dimensions, but a statistical artifact created by ipsatization, then the reasoning presented throughout this book about the kinds of conflicts that generate values is wrong. Fortunately, empirical evidence supports the bipolar position. *A principal components analysis of the raw, unipsatized three societies value data yields exactly the same bipolar dimensions as the ipsatized data after the first component has been removed.* Thus the second, third, and fourth dimensions of the raw, unipsatized data show the same bipolar structure as the first three dimensions of the ipsatized data. It is true, as Schimmack et al. point out, that the *individualism* versus *collectivism* and *altruism* versus *self-interest* are not formed by contradictory opposites such as *up* and *down*. But, to repeat the point made earlier, this does not mean that they are not dimensions. As dimensions they are formed by the correlational structure of semantic contraries (things opposed in nature or tendency) rather than contradictories (whatever is true of one is logically false about the other).

Political Attitudes and the Circumplex

To explore the usefulness of this dimensional analysis in understanding American politics, I reanalyzed selected data from the 1988 Gallup study of the American electorate (Ornstein et al. 1988). In this study the authors clustered Americans into groups (*enterprisers, moralists, upbeats, disaffecteds, bystanders, and followers, seculars, 1960s' democrats, new dealers*, and *passive poor* and *partisan poor*) on the basis of a variety of attitude measures and demographic characteristics. In their report they present a number of tables in which percentages—percent republican, percent pro-union, percent strongly favoring the idea that women should return to their more traditional role, and so on—are given for each of the groups. Because they have used the same groups across tables it is possible to create a new table combining the percentages of many different variables for these groups. From such a table it is possible not only to analyze the relations of the groups to each of the variables, but also to relate the variables to each other. A special scaling technique, called *correspondence analysis*, is especially appropriate for this task (Weller and Romney 1990). Correspondence analysis is a variety of principal components analysis in which a rectangular data array is subjected to single-value decomposition after normalizing both rows and columns. Correspondence analysis has the advantage of being able to place both rows and columns in the same space. It is one of the current techniques of choice for the descriptive modeling of tabled frequency data.

Twenty-seven variables from various tables in the Gallup report were selected and a correspondence analysis carried out after normalizing columns and rows of the data. The results are presented in figure 5.3. The groups are labeled in italics. The terms in italics have been added on the basis of my interpretation of the dimensions involved. One important aspect of the results of this analysis is that it provides some evidence that the political world is organized by the same value dimensions of *individualism* versus *collectivism* and *altruism* versus *self-interest*. The correspondence analysis helps clear up some of the confusions between liberalism and individualism, and between collectivism and conservatism. Liberalism contains not just individualistic values, but also strong altruistic values, such as protecting the environment. And conservatism contains not just collectivistic values, but also strong self-interest values, including a high value on the military and promotion of business values. Overall, the *altruism* versus *self-interest* and *individualism* versus *communalism* dimensions would seem to be more fundamental than the *conservative* versus *liberal* dimension, since they are found universally, not just in Western societies, and are not tied to specific political issues. It is interesting that the term *libertarian* is becoming a more frequently used political term. In figure 5.3 libertarians would be on the private enterprise line—libertarians are those individualists who believe in the freedom to be entirely selfish if it does not hurt anyone else, like the freedom to sell one's own body parts. While at present there does not seem to be much political analysis with respect to the two basic value dimensions outlined earlier, the circumplex framework presented here may prove useful in accounting for a variety of internal value tensions within both Democrat and Republican parties.

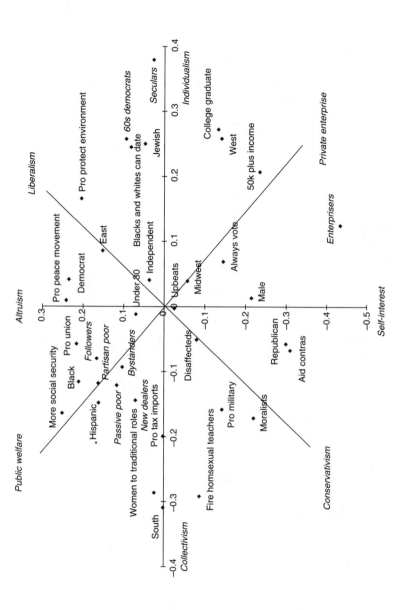

Figure 5.3 Correspondence analysis of political issues: selected data from Ornstein et al. (1988).

What Is *Collectivism* Really?

A two-dimensional analysis of the sort provided here is useful in disentangling some of the disputes about the nature of collectivism and individualism. Some of these disputes occur because different analysts place the theoretical axes of their definitions of *individualism* and *collectivism* at different angles around the circumplex. Other disputes occur because different clusters of items are taken to be the features of either pole. For example, Oyserman et al. find that the elements used to define *individualism* greatly affect the degree of difference found between Americans and Japanese. In their meta-analysis they find that Americans are higher in *individualism* than Japanese if, in addition to personal independence, items having to do with uniqueness, privacy, and direct communication are included. But if these items are not included, then Americans are lower in *individualism* than the Japanese. Oyserman et al. also found that while Americans are generally less *collectivistic* than other societies, American are more likely to have higher *collectivism* ratings than other societies when the measure of *collectivism* includes items about the importance of belonging to in-groups and seeking others' advice. Comparing Americans to the Japanese they find that Americans are higher in *collectivism* than the Japanese on most *collectivism* scales (!), but not when the *collectivism* scales include items referring to preference for working in groups and exclude items relating to striving to maintain group harmony. With respect to the role the family and *collectivism*, Oyserman et al. found no consensus among the 27 scales they examined on whether or not family items will be included in a *collectivism* scale. Surprisingly, Oyserman et al. find that in studies in which the *collectivism* scale focuses on family obligations, Americans tend to be more collectivistic than either the Chinese or Japanese.

All this demonstrates that *collectivism* and *individualism* as orientations are not tight, highly coherent entities. *Thus, the average correlation between specific collectivism items is only 0.18, and the average correlation between individualism items is only 0.13.* These low correlations do not mean that there is no dimension of *individualism* versus *collectivism*, but they do indicate that *individualism* versus *collectivism* is an entity without much entitivity. If someone says that society A is higher on *collectivism* than society B, little has really been said until one knows the items that have been included in the measurement of *collectivism*. It is interesting that the same problem arises when respondents are interviewed in depth. Claudia Strauss reports, for example, that careful analysis of the statements of particular individuals shows that various elements of individualistic and collectivistic orientations are organized in people's minds in quite complex ways that do not fit onto a single dimension. It could be that no single individual's structure perfectly fits the simple bipolar structure given here (Strauss 2000). The best recommendation is to present data concerning the items and clusters by which individual societies differ, not just dimensional differences.

Industriousness versus *Relaxation*

The third dimension in table 5.1 is labeled *industriousness* versus *relaxation*. Like the first two dimensions, the opposite ends of the pole are contraries (e.g., *industry* versus *relaxation*) rather than contradictories (e.g., *industry* versus *sloth*). *The being a leader* cluster had lesser but significant loadings on the *self-interest* dimension while the *pursuing knowledge* cluster had lesser but significant loadings on the *individualism* dimension. The macro cluster of *amusements* on the *relaxation* side of the dimension also showed a slight but distinct pattern of positive loadings on *individualism* and negative loadings on *altruism*. The strongest loadings on this dimension belong to the *diligence* macro cluster and the *having high standards* cluster.

As we shall see, the three societies are similar on both poles of this dimension; *industry* is rated highly, *relaxation* is not. The *industry* versus *relaxation* dimension is a potential candidate for cultural universality. However, despite the high value Americans, Japanese, and Vietnamese place on work, diligence, having high standards, and the like, it may be that this dimension as a dimension disappears in nonindustrialized nations. It does not seem to be an important value orientation in the world of Jane Austen or the Kalahari of Nisa. It may be that the modern world creates the kind of conflict that produces such a value orientation; a world in which the amount of work one does is something that—in part—one takes on oneself.

Brief Remarks on Faux Causality

Apart from the many problems of measurement, there are special conceptual problems in the way many social scientists think about values. One such conceptual problem is the problem of *faux causality*. For example, sometimes social scientists say that the collectivist standards found in a particular society are caused by the fact that the society is collectivistic. This is faux causality, because one is claiming that the existence of something is caused by the thing itself. Faux causality is both a common confusion and often-used rhetorical strategy in the social sciences; terms such as *culture* and *social structure* and *personality* are examples *par excellence. Culture*, for example, is said to consist of shared ideas and meanings and attitudes and values and practices and discourses, and then the ideas and meanings of a particular society are explained by saying they are caused by the *culture* of that society. Faux causality allows the social scientist to present descriptions as if they were explanations. This is an especially egregious problem in the study of value orientations, which are too often presented as both description and cause.

Chapter 6

Similarities and Differences

Figure 6.1 presents a bar graph for each of the 58 clusters for each of the three societies organized by dimension. The high degree of agreement between societies is visually apparent. (This same agreement can be seen in more detail in the appendix) The mean r for the intercorrelation of the three societies for the clusters on the *individualism* versus *collectivism* dimension is 0.52. For the clusters on the *altruism* versus *self-interest* dimension the mean r is 0.79. For the clusters on the *industry* versus *relaxation* dimension the mean $r = 0.89$. The Vietnamese display the greatest value differences but only for the *collectivism* versus *individualism* differences. For the other two dimensions the three societies show a mean intercorrelation of 0.84.

Although there is a high degree of similarity between societies, this does not mean that there are no differences in values between societies. *T* tests for each pair of societies for all the clusters show that societies that are different from each other by just 0.2 on the scale at the top of the bar graphs will be statistically significant at the 0.05 probability level. Seventy-three percent of the 174 *t* tests are statistically significant at the 0.05 level. Thus the majority of these small differences are not due to random chance.

The visual comparison of the bar graphs in figure 6.1 illustrates the high degree of agreement between societies on values. A more quantitative method developed by Romney and his associates can be used to determine not only the strength of agreement between societies, but also the amount of agreement that is unique to each society (Romney et al. 1997; Moore et al. 1999). This direct comparison of intercultural to intra-cultural variability makes possible a quantitative analysis of both cultural similarity *and* cultural difference. This method is based on the partitioning of the agreement of respondents from the same society into two components; the first due to their agreement with what is common across all societies (the universal heritage), the second due to agreement with what is specific to each society (the unique cultural heritage). The two together combine to form the agreement *within* a society.

	Americans	Japanese	Vietnamese
	Below av | Above av	Below av | Above av	Below av | Above av
	−1.0 −0.5 0 0.5 1.0	−1.0 −0.5 0 0.5 1.0	−1.0 −0.5 0 0.5 1.0

Individualism
Self-fulfillment	|====: ===	|====: ==	| ===
Choosing my own goals	|====: =	|====	| ==
Being optimistic	|====:	|====	| ===
Being relaxed and enjoying life	|====: =	|====: =	|
Feeling sure about myself	|====: =	|====	| =
Being creative	|====	|====	=|
Being open to change	|====:	|====	=|
Having love and satisfying sex	|====	|==	==|
Having time alone	|=	|===	===|
Having fun	|====: =	=|	====|
Understanding science	|	|=	|
Liking art and literature	===|	==|	=: ====|
Living a life of adventure	|	===|	===: ====|
Right to abortion, gay rights, etc.	=|	====|	==: ====: ====|
Resisting authority	=: ====|	==: ====|	===: ====|

Collectivism
Being respectful and polite	|==	|====	|====: ==
Having a close-knit family	|==	|	|====:
Being thrifty	=|	|==	|===
Being sexual restrained	|	=|	|===
Defending my country	====|	==|	|====:
Having law & social order	====|	===|	|===
Maintaining tradition	====|	==|	|=
Being careful	====|	=|	|
Working for the group etc.	===: ====|	===: ====|	|=
The military, death sentence.	===: ====|	=: ====|	=|
Being religious	: ====: ====|	−1.5	====|

Altruism
Being honest and genuine	|====: ===	|====: ==	|====: ===
Avoiding war	|====	|====: ====: =	|====: ==
Respecting others feelings	|====	|====: =	|====
Treating people equally	|====	|====: =	|====
Finding meaning in life	|==	|====	|====:
Having close friends	|====	|====:	|=
Living in harmony with nature	|=	|====:	|=
Being able to adust	|=	|====	|
Controlling myself	|=	|=	|
Working for social improvement	|=	=|	|=
Public schools, the UN	==|	|	|=

Self-interest
Being prosperous	|=	=|	|===
Keeping fit	|=	|=	|==
Being liked and belonging	|	==|	|
Being ambitious & competitive	==|	===|	: ====|
Market competition	==: ====|	=|	|
Having nice things	====|	===|	: ====|
Having social status	==: ====|	===: ====|	: ====|

Industry
Being persistent	|====: =	|====: =	|====
Being responsible	|====	|====	|====:
Planning for the future	|====	|====	|====:
Being practical & realistic	|====	|===	|===
Pursuing knowledge	|====	|====	|==
Having high standards	|====:	|=	|===
Working hard	|===	|	|===
Being orderly and regular	|	|=	|=
Being a leader	|	=: ====|	=|

Relaxation
Sleeping, eating, drinking alcohol	==|	|===	=: ====|
Watching movies, tv, eating out	===: ====|	=: ====|	====: ====|
Believing in omens, etc.	=: ====|	=: ====|	====: ====|
Enjoying comics, board games, etc.	====: ====|	=: ====: ====|	=: ====: ====|
Being detached etc.	==: ====: ====|	==: ====|	====|

Figure 6.1 Value cluster means for Americans, Japanese, and Vietnamese.

Agreement within a society = agreement common to all societies
+ agreement specific to that society

To find the degree of agreement common to all three societies three between-society correlation matrices are calculated; the matrix of correlations for each respondent in the American sample with each respondent in the Japanese sample, the matrix for the correlations of the American respondents with Vietnamese respondents, and the matrix for the correlations of the Japanese respondents with the Vietnamese respondents. The mean r for the correlation matrix of the American sample and Japanese sample is 0.32, for the American sample and Vietnamese sample 0.19, and 0.22 for the Japanese sample and Vietnamese sample. The average of these three coefficients is 0.24. This represents the average agreement of respondents *not* from the same society and hence the common agreement.

The next step is to transform these coefficients into sharing estimates of cultural sharing. To calculate this we take the square root of the correlation between individuals. The rationale behind the square root transformation can be illustrated with a genetic model. Consider the agreement in height between half-sisters who have the same father. The expected correlation in heights between half-sisters is 0.25. It is 0.25 because for each pair of sisters, sister A received 50 percent of her genes from her father and sister B received 50 percent of her genes from the same father; and 50 percent of 50 percent is 25 percent. If we take the square root of 0.25, we get 0.50, which is the proportion of genes each sister shares with her father. Now imagine values as genes. We assume that people agree with each other in values because they share a common heritage. Since the respondents from the three different societies are correlated, on the average, 0.24 with each other in their value judgments, then they must, on the average, be correlated 0.49—the square root of 0.24—with whatever is their common heritage.

The next step is to calculate the degree of agreement found within the three societies. To compute this for a particular society, we calculate the average correlation between respondents within the same society (not counting the diagonals), which represents the total sum of agreement between respondents. For the American sample the mean r is 0.38, for the Japanese 0.42, and for the Vietnamese 0.32. The average of the three is 0.37. Given a mean r of 0.37, the amount each person shares with the common heritage within societies, on the average, is the square root of 0.37, or 0.61. This means 61 percent of the average respondent's judgments can be accounted for as due to the effect of the common heritage found within societies However, we have calculated that 49 percent of this total is due to the common agreement among the three societies. The difference between the two percentages—61 percent minus 49 percent, or 12 percent—is the proportion of sharing that is due to the unique aspect of the culture for each of the three societies.

The structure of the consensus model is as follows:

Person by person correlations between societies

	Japanese	Vietnamese	Americans
Japanese	–	–	–
Vietnamese	0.21	–	–
Americans	0.32	0.19	–

Mean r between societies = 0.24

The average agreement across societies is the square root of 0.24 = 0.49 or 49 percent

Person by person correlations *within* societies

	Japanese	Vietnamese	Americans
Japanese	0.41	–	–
Vietnamese	–	0.38	–
Americans	–	–	0.31

Mean r within societies = 0.37

The average agreement within society is the square root of 0.37 = 0.61

Average agreement due to the *unique heritage* of each society *equals* the average agreement of the within society heritage minus the average agreement across societies.

$$0.61 - 0.49 = 0.12 \text{ or } 12 \text{ percent}$$

Proportion of individual judgments not due to either *the unique heritage* of each society or the universal heritage (individual differences) equals 1.0 minus the average agreement due to the *unique heritage* plus *the universal heritage*:

$$1.0 - (0.49 + 0.12) = 0.39 \text{ or } 39 \text{ percent}$$

These results indicate that cultural differences in values are small (12 percent) compared to overall similarity across societies (49 percent). Using the cultural consensus model, the overall agreement of the three societies with each other is more than *four* times larger than unique cultural effects. Schwartz and Bardi (2001) took the data set collected by Schwartz and his associates and examined the correlation between the averages of specific nations with the overall average for all nations. The total sample, collected over 10 years, included teachers in 56 nations, college students in 54 nations, and near-representative samples for 13 nations, involving all in all more than 30,000 respondents with translations of the Schwartz value survey into 39 languages. Schwartz and Bardi grouped their specific items into 10 value types. They then calculated the overall average for each kind of sample (representative, teacher, students) for the 10 types, and correlated the overall averages with the means for each nation (taking out of the overall averages in each case the means for that nation.) The results were consistent across types of samples and regions of the world. For the representative samples, the mean r across nations was 0.92. For teachers the mean r was 0.90, and students the mean r was 0.91.

Schwartz and Bardi's results are even stronger than the results reported earlier, perhaps because Schwartz and Bardi have grouped their specific items into a small number of types or clusters. When items are grouped, correlations with the grand average tend to increase because grouping pools common variance. A computer simulation experiment indicates that this effect is quite general, although the size of the increase of the correlations of groups of items to the common standard compared to the correlation of individual items to the common standard varies in complex ways as the different variance components change in size. However, whether the figures in this book or the Schwartz and Bardi figures are used, the conclusion stays the same; there is a strong agreement across societies about values. These results may seem startling, but similar results have been found for cross-cultural data in other domains. For example, in a study of the semantics of emotion terms for Americans, Chinese, and Japanese, Moore et al. found 54 percent agreement with the between-society or universal heritage, 15 percent due to culturally unique heritages, and 31 percent due to individual differences and noise.

One caveat is in order here Agreement in the consensus analysis model is measured by correlation coefficients. Correlation coefficients are a good measure of the similarity of things with respect to their *profiles*. If one had a small clay model of the Rocky Mountains, the correlation between the peaks of mountains in the real world and in the clay model (if the model was carefully made) could be perfect—an *r* of 1.00. But the actual distances between the peak of a mountain in the clay model and a peak of the same mountain in the real world would be thousands of feet. The Pearson *r* does not measure how far apart the matching data points are, only the degree to which the points have similar profiles. But this is not a problem if the two variables have similar means and similar standard deviations because then similarity in the profile will also measure similarity in distance.

Thus, there is a question about whether the similarity in profiles, as measured by the correlation coefficients used in the consensus model, also gives a good sense of the distances between scores from different societies. This is impossible to answer with the ipsatized data because each person's scores have been normalized to a mean of zero and a standard deviation of one, wiping out the distance differences between individuals. So, in order to explore the relation between distances and profile it is necessary to return to the raw data. In general, the means for individuals are similar for the three societies; for the raw data the American respondents have an overall mean of 2.68, the Japanese respondents 2.41, and the Vietnamese respondents 2.85. The standard deviations for each society are almost identical; the Americans 1.10, the Japanese 1.11, and the Vietnamese 1.18. These figures show that mean elevations for each society are reasonably close—within a fourth of a standard deviation of each other. The best guess is that this difference reflects some general tendency for the people in the different societies to use the Likert scales differently, with the Vietnamese using the upper end of the five-point scales more than the Japanese, rather than reflecting real differences in values.

The Universal Pattern

These results raise the question: What is the shared universal value pattern? Of course, the term *universal* needs caveats since the sample is only three societies, and even including Schwartz and Bardi's 56 nations, tribal peoples are not represented. But, given the caveats, what do the data say? Looking at figure 6.1, it can be seen that some of the *individualism* clusters have a mixed profile, but *the self-fulfillment, choosing own goals,* and being *optimistic* clusters are above average for all three societies. The clusters *living a life of adventure, resisting authority,* and *sexual freedom* have below average ratings. It would seem *individualism* is good unless it gets too close to disorder.

For the Americans and Japanese, *collectivism* clusters tend toward below average ratings, but are predominately above average for the Vietnamese. The *being religious* cluster is below average for all three societies. The *death sentence, military*, and *national security* clusters are also primarily negative. The predominately positive clusters are *having a family* and *being respectful and polite*.

The *altruism* clusters are predominately above average. The top items from the 328 values are *treating human life as precious* and *following my conscience and doing right*. The clusters *treating people equally, respecting other's feelings, being honest and genuine, having close friends, avoiding war*, and *living in harmony with nature* all have strongly above average ratings. Everywhere, it seems, it is good to be good, and to be good typically means treating others well.

In contrast, the world of *self-interest* receives low ratings. Although people want—and know they want—money, status, and nice things, people say that it is not these things that they *value* most highly. Items dealing with financial security have above average ratings unless the amount of money is large. The clusters *having social status* and *having nice things* clusters are below average. *Self-advancement* and *market competition*, also strong, tend to be below average. The universal value pattern seems to treat acquisition of power, position, or things as basically selfish, and hence not admirable.

The same general pattern is found with respect to *industry*. The clusters *having high standards, pursuing knowledge, being persistent, working hard, being responsible. planning for the future*, and *being practical* are all above average. But the *being a leader* cluster tends to be below average, and quite low in Japan. Finally, the items *relaxation* clusters are all below average except for above an average rating on sleeping, eating, drinking alcohol, and so on, in Japan. Pleasure without redeeming social value is not as good and important as work.

A check on these conclusions comes from the already cited work of Schwartz and Bardi. In their paper they present the pan-cultural results for their 10 value types. Table 6.1 compares the Three Society data with the Schwartz and Bardi data, matching the specific items from the Three Society questionnaire with the specific items used to form the Schwartz and Bardi types. In most cases the matches are quite close. (The means have been normalized for both studies to facilitate comparison.) The level of agreement is high; the group means correlate 0.95. The Schwartz and Bardi results are an impressive demonstration of the pan-cultural value profile, with its high evaluation of treating others well and being self-directed and its lower evaluation of wealth, power, and personal pleasures.

Table 6.1 Comparison between Schwartz value data and American, Japanese, and Vietnamese value data

Schwartz Types with Specific Items	American, Japanese, and Vietnamese Matching Items
Normalized cluster mean	*Normalized Cluster mean*
1.2 Benevolence	*1.2 Benevolence*
Helpful	Taking care of others
Honest	Being honest and genuine
Forgiving	Forgiving others
Loyal	Being loyal to my friends
Responsible	Being responsible
0.9 Self-direction	*1.2 Self-direction*
Creativity	Being creative
Freedom	(None)
Independent	Being independent and self-
Curious	reliant
Choosing Own goals	Being interested in many things
0.8 Universalism	Choosing my own goals
Broad minded	*0.7 Universalism*
Wisdom	Accepting people as they are
Social justice	Gaining experience and wisdom
Equality	from suffering
A world at peace	Working for social justice
A world of beauty	Treating people equally
Unity with nature	Avoiding war
0.6 Security	Enjoying the beauty of nature
Family security	Living in harmony with nature
National security	*0.3 Security*
Social order	Fulfilling family obligations
Clean	Defending my country
Reciprocation of favors	Law and order
0.5 Conformity	(None)
Obedient	(None)
Politeness	*0.6 Conformity*
Self-discipline	Being obedient
Honoring parents & elders	Being polite and well mannered
0.1 Achievement	Holding myself to high
Successful	standards
Capable	Having deep respect for parents
Ambitious	and grandparents
Influential	*−0.3 Achievement*
−0.4 Hedonism	Being a success
Pleasure	Being competent and effective
Enjoying life	Being ambitious
	Being important

Continued

Table 6.1 Continued

Schwartz Types with Specific Items	*American, Japanese, and Vietnamese Matching Items*
−1.1 *Stimulation*	0.2 *Hedonism*
Daring	Having erotic pleasure
A varied life	Enjoying life
An exciting life	−1.0 *Stimulation*
−0.9 *Tradition*	Taking risks
Humble	Traveling to new places
Accepting my portion in life	Living a life of adventure
Devout	−1.1 *Tradition*
Respect for tradition	Respecting authority
Moderate	Accepting one's fate
−1.8 *Power*	Having strong religious faith
Social power	Maintaining old traditions
Authority	Being careful and avoiding
Wealth	unnecessary risks
Preserving my public image	−1.7 *Power*
	Being one of the elite
	Having authority over others
	Having great wealth
	Having others think well of me
r *between cluster means 0.95*	

A Note on Sample Size

The understanding of what constitutes an appropriate sample size varies greatly by sub-field. In some areas of biology, results from one nematode can be considered powerful evidence about all animals. In contrast, in some areas of social survey research, sample sizes under 2,000 or 3,000 are unacceptable. It is well known that part of the answer to how many subjects are needed for a study depends on the size of the effect one wishes to measure. If one wants to know within two standard errors the American vote within one-half a percent, a representative sample of 40,000 will be needed, but if one wants to know the vote within 10 percent, a sample of 100 is sufficient.

However, there is more to the sample size issue than just fixing confidence intervals. Consider the effect of agreement between the subjects for a given domain. If one has no reason to believe that what is true of one respondent's answers is true for another, then one is in the world of independent judgments and the standard statistical model of independent judgments applies. But if one has reason to think that what is true for one subject is likely to be true for another, than the model of independent judgments no longer applies. This appears to be the case with values. Schwartz and Bardi find that their 10 value types correlate, on the average, 0.90, with the pan-national standard. This means that one needs only a small number of nations to obtain a good estimate of pan-national standards. Consider a hypothetical case in which for some domain, national averages are correlated 1.00 with the pan-national average. How many societies would it take to estimate the pan-national average? Obviously, just one. The Schwartz and Bardi correlation of 0.90 is not far from 1.00. Mathematically, one can expect that if one takes three societies at random and if one averages their value profiles, the averaged profile for three societies will correlate with the pan-national average above 0.95. In this case just three societies can be expected to give an excellent estimate of the pan-national or universal value profile.

Chapter 7

The Americans

The Sample

The American sample consisted of students from the University of California, San Diego. Most of the questionnaires were handed out from tables near an area where undergraduates congregate between classes. Students were paid for their participation. Sixty-six percent of the sample were women. Seventy percent were native Californians. The mean age was 23. From the information given about occupation, years of education, and income, estimates of each respondent's Socio-Economic Status (SES) were calculated using a coding system specially developed for this purpose. Seventy-seven of the respondents were SES I, 62 SES II, 47 SES III, 14 SES IV, and 10 SES 10. Based on the high number of SES I respondents, it seems likely that a number of the respondents represented their parents as having more prestigious occupations than they in fact held. Mean yearly parental income was slightly more than $100,000. Father's mean years of education was just under 17. Self-defined religious affiliations are given in table 7.1.

In general, the American sample seems representative of students at a large state research university.

What's Special about Americans?

Although the variance accounted for by unique cultural components is not large, this unique part is nevertheless interesting. But from a graph like figure 5.1 it is difficult to determine the unique part of a society's values because the salience of the common pattern makes differences difficult to detect. One technique for locating distinctive items when, on the average, group differences are small, is to examine just the highest rated items. A statistical fact, well known in the test and measurement field, is that the top 5 percent of the scores on one variable will show little or no correlation with the top 5 percent from another variable even when the variables are highly correlated because

Table 7.1   Religious denominations:
American sample

Denomination	Frequency
Presbyterian	4
Episcopalian	3
Catholic	49
Mormon	4
Christian	31
Baptist	5
Jewish	19
Hindu	4
Buddhist	9
None	65
Other	16

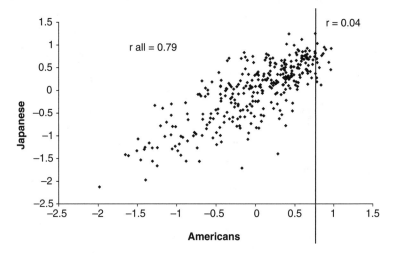

Figure 7.1   Scatter plot for Americans and Japanese 328 value items.

of the large scatter around the regression line. For example, taking
the top 20 American values, and correlating the ratings for just these
items with the matching 20 Japanese items, the correlation between
the two is only 0.04, although the correlation for all 328 items is 0.79.
Figure 7.1 gives the scatter plot for the American and Japanese 328
value items. The lack of correlation between Americans and Japanese
values for the top 20 items is apparent.

The top 10 items for each of the 3 societies show very little overlap. These results are presented in table 7.2. For Americans, these top values have a distinctly American character, showing a complex balance between individual satisfactions (*enjoying life, having a personally fulfilling life*), self-determination (*choosing my own goals, being independent,* and *self-reliant*), affective social relatedness (*having love, having someone I can really talk to, finding a mate with good qualities*), and virtue (*being a good person, being true to myself*). Equally distinctive on the cultural level are the Vietnamese items concerning family and appropriate behavior and the Japanese items concerning avoiding war and having close friends. As anecdotal evidence it is interesting that when the list of top American values is read to undergraduates, they sometimes spontaneously remark that this is a good summary of their own personal values.

The fact that top value items tend to be unique may help to explain the genesis of the belief that cultures have very different values. The natural tendency to notice things that are different in a foreign society

Table 7.2 Top 10 of 328 value items: Americans, Japanese, and Vietnamese

Rank	Americans	Japanese	Vietnamese
1	Enjoying life	Being healthy	Having deep respect for parents and grandpa
2	Being a good person	Avoiding war	Taking care of my parents when they get old
3	Having a personally fulfilling life	Treating human life as precious	Treating human life as precious
4	Having love	Having close supportive friends	Following my conscience and doing right
5	Having someone I can really talk to	Having a world free of war	Not dishonoring my family
6	Choosing my own goals	Making friends	Fulfilling family obligations
7	Being true to myself	Having someone I can really talk to	Being employed
8	Finding a mate with good qualities	Having a positive outlook on life	Being healthy
9	Having wisdom	Enjoying life	Being responsible
10	Being independent and self-reliant	Having love	Having a secure job

would be greatly reinforced by the fact that the most salient values in a society tend to be unique. The salience of a society's very top values, reflected again and again in conversation, argument, and sermon, understandably blinds the observer to the fact that if the whole range of human values is taken into account when societies are compared, most societies are very similar.

While the top value items are informative, they constitute only a small portion of the data. As a method to include all the data, the averages for each society can be compared with the Three Society averages. Figure 7.2 presents a bar graph showing the differences by clusters for the American sample compared to the Three Society average.

Two general conclusions can be drawn from figure 7.2. The first is that Americans are more *individualistic* and somewhat less *collectivistic* than the other two societies. The second is that Americans are not very different from the other two societies with respect to *altruism* and *industry*. There is significant tendency for Americans to value *industry* slightly more than the overall average, but the size of the effect is less than a quarter of a standard deviation—in terms of human height, a difference of about 3/4 of an inch. Testing was carried out before 9/11, so the American evaluation of *avoiding war* may have changed, although the direction the shift may have taken is not obvious. The low rating of the American sample for *market competition, economic growth*, and *capitalism* seem to reflect a lack of enthusiasm about the business world that is part of campus culture in many American colleges and universities.

A useful technique to help in understanding these low ratings is to examine the correlations of these items with all the other items in each society. The results are presented in table 7.3. To construct table 7.3 the correlations of the 328 specific items with *market competition, economic growth*, and *capitalism* for each society were calculated, and then averaged across these 4 items. The top 13 items with the highest averages have been informally grouped to help in interpretation.

The results in table 7.3 show that for Americans, *market competition, capitalism*, and *economic growth* are correlated with nationalism, business, and democracy. The Japanese, in contrast, associate *market competition, capitalism*, and *economic growth* with social striving and being industrious, as well as being optimistic and creative. The Vietnamese, in turn, have a more Fordist set of associations to social planning and mastery of nature, as well as associations to liberalism and nationalism. Thus the American results appear to be part of a general pattern of a low evaluation of national institutions.

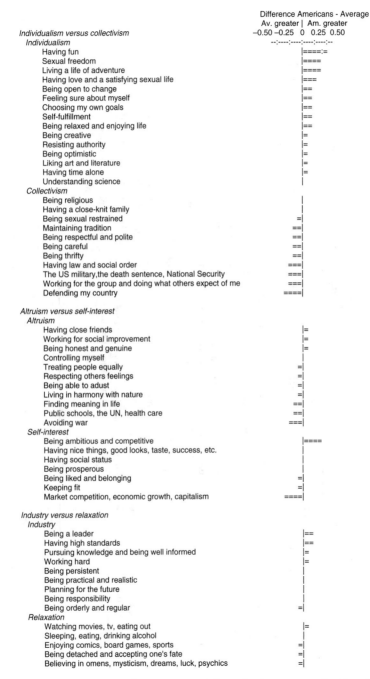

Figure 7.2 Comparison of Americans to Three Society average for 58 value clusters.

Table 7.3 Top 20 average correlations with average for *market competition, capitalism, and economic growth*

American	r	Japanese	r	Vietnamese	r
Being loyal to my country	0.25	Having social status	0.22	Social planning	0.32
The U.S. military	0.22	Being a success	0.20	Organizing and coordinating activities	0.16
Defending my country	0.22	Having others think well of me	0.18	Law and order	0.16
My country	0.16	Not losing face	0.16		
Maintaining national security	0.16	Not being poor	0.20	Science	0.26
Making good a profit	0.24	Having business skills	0.22	Maintaining a sustainable environment	0.26
Having business skills	0.22	Getting tasks done right away	0.17	Conquering nature	0.20
Being prosperous	0.17	Being competitive	0.16		
Owning a good stereo, a nice car, house	0.16	Being a leader	0.19	Being loyal to my country	0.23
Democracy	0.22	Being optimistic	0.21	Defending my country	0.23
Having a well-organized society	0.21	Being creative	0.17	The U.S. military	0.20
Law and order	0.20	Doing what others expect me to	0.21	Maintaining national security	0.20
Government based on laws	0.18	Maintaining national security	0.19	Liberal political policies	0.19
				Government based on laws	0.18
				The elimination of racism	0.16

Returning to the graph in figure 7.2 portraying the value differences between Americans and other societies, certain issues need to be raised. A major drawback in using this type of graph is that it presents a distorted representation of a society's values. For example, the graph does not indicate the high value of *being honest and genuine*, or *being persistent*, typical of Americans, because these results are also typical of most societies. Usually values are not thought of as they are depicted in figure 7.2. To say some society values *being persistent*, for instance, typically means that *being persistent* is valued highly relative to other *values*, not other *societies*.

This baseline problem may have caused much of the ambiguity and confusion in the literature about the nature of American values. The attempts by Albert, DuBois, Gillin, the Kluckhohns, Spindler, Williams and others to describe American values lacked a clearly defined cross-cultural referential baseline. What each analyst found as salient in the United States was thought to be distinctive of the United States. But, in retrospect, it can be seen that a great deal of what they described was not distinctive at all. American values of initiative, self-determination, honesty, self-fulfillment, hard work, and egalitarianism are typical of most nations, not just Americans.

Comparative quantitative research results on values did not occur until the 1980s with the pioneering work of Hofstede, Triandis, and Schwartz. In the period from 1950 to the 1980s most value research was carried out in just one society, usually the United States. Even in the United States it was not until Rokeach's work in 1970s that systematic ratings of a reasonably large sample of value items became available. Thus early research on values suffered from the lack of an empirically derived cross-cultural baseline to compare societies cross-culturally as well as the lack of systematic rating methods that could permit comparison of one value with another within a society. Not surprisingly, these early characterizations of American values lacked consensual validation—each analyst had a different unstated baseline resulting in different impressions of American values. No method existed by which they could come to agreement.

Pluralistic Ignorance and the Typical American

When these results have been presented to social scientists in colloquia and lectures, a common reaction has been open disbelief. Americans, it is said, value money and prestige and success. The

American data was too nice. The supporting evidence from Schwartz and Bardi (2001) and from Rokeachs's 1968 and 1971 NORC value survey (Rokeach and Ball-Rokeach 1989) does not impress these critics. It was interesting that the objectors agreed that they themselves, and most of their friends, valued being honest and being good to others more than they valued wealth or power, but they believed most Americans were not like them. In order to explore this phenomenon further, a questionnaire was constructed using the same items and the same format as the Three Society value questionnaire, which asked respondents to rate the 328 items the way a "typical American" would ("Rate how much the typical American values the following items"). The results are presented in figure 7.3.

The differences between respondents' idea of the *typical* American and their self-ratings can be easily summarized: Compared to their ratings for themselves, Americans think *typical* Americans *value having social status, nice things, being liked and belonging* much more than they do, but value being *egalitarian* and *honest* much less. Americans also think the *typical* American values *movies and sports and entertainments* more than they do, and values being *industrious* and *responsible* somewhat less. The story for *collectivism* is more complex; Americans think the *typical* American values the patriotic, nationalistic, religious side of *collectivism* more than they do, but values the familial and well-mannered side of *collectivism* less. Finally, *typical* Americans are seen as less *individualistic* with regard to *openness* and *optimism*. The correlation of the 328 item value profile for *typical* Americans correlates only 0.32 with the actual American profile. Thus Americans are more like the Japanese and the Vietnamese than they are like the Americans of their imagination.

It is interesting that Americans display such pluralistic ignorance of the shared values of their own society; everyone believes that they live in a world in which they are better than the others. At this point there does not appear to be typicality data for other societies; it is not known if this degree of collective ignorance is a general phenomenon or something special to Americans. Later some speculative reasons for why people distort in this way will be presented, but at this point in the story it is one more puzzling finding that was not anticipated.

Religion

In all three societies, items relating to religion were given below average ratings. In figure 7.3, it can be seen that no items in the religion

Figure 7.3 Comparison of Americans to the "Typical American" for 58 value clusters.

cluster had above average ratings. *Being guided by religious scriptures* and *doing what God wants me to* averaged a standard deviation below the mean value rating, and even *observing religious holidays* is almost a standard deviation below the mean. These results would seem to indicate a sample bias given the importance that religion currently plays on the American political scene and the renaissance of evangelical Christianity. The American sample of college students seems even more secular than the average undergraduate (Sax et al. 2003) According to these studies, over 60 percent of Freshmen pray once or more times a week and approximately 80 percent attended religious services frequently or occasionally when they were in High School.

Turning to the American data, and cross-tabulating respondents' self-identification of religious affiliation with the specific items in the *being religious* cluster, presented in table 7.4, most of the religious groups are average or below average in their value ratings for the five specific items. For the American sample the overall impression is that religion is a conventional value, not strongly internalized except by members of special denominations. The specific item *being religious* is rated by those stating a religious denomination about as highly as *understanding science, being different from others*, and *having good taste*.

Schwartz and Huismans carried out a study of the relation of values to religiosity among Spanish Roman Catholics, Dutch Calvinist Protestants, Israel Jews, and Greek Orthodox respondents (Schwartz and Huismans 1995). Respondents answered the Schwartz value survey and an eight-point religiosity scale ranging from not at all religious (0) to very religious (7). The Israeli Jews had the lowest religiosity mean score of 1.7, followed by the Spanish Roman Catholics (2.5), Greek Orthodox (3.4), and Dutch Protestants (4.6). For all four groups the religiosity score correlated positively with the Schwartz value types that are aligned on the *collectivism* pole (*tradition,*

Table 7.4 American mean ratings for the *religion* cluster

Having strong religious faith	0.4	0.3	−0.1	−0.2	−0.5	−0.3	−0.4	−1.3	−1.8	−0.4
Observing religious holidays	0.4	0.1	0.1	−0.2	−0.4	−1.0	−1.0	−0.5	−1.5	−0.4
Doing what God wants me to	0.3	0.0	0.2	0.0	−0.6	−0.8	−1.2	−1.9	−1.8	−0.7
Being religious	0.1	−0.4	−0.1	0.0	−0.7	−0.7	−1.3	−1.0	−1.9	−0.7
Being guided by religious scriptures	0.4	0.3	−0.4	−0.6	−0.9	−1.0	−0.8	−1.6	−2.1	−0.8
Average	0.3	0.1	−0.1	−0.2	−0.6	−0.8	−0.9	−1.3	−1.8	

security, and *conformity*), and negatively with the value types on the *individualism* pole (*self-direction, hedonism,* and *stimulation*). These results support the cross-society generalization that religious and other collectivist values are moderately highly correlated.

It is difficult to find information in the research literature specifically targeted to measure the strength and depth of religious values in the American population. There are a large number of studies concerning church attendance and prayer, but such surveys do not measure the psychological depth of the respondent's involvement with religion. One exception is the research of Kenneth Kendler, a psychiatrist interested in twins and mental health (Kendler et al. 2003), Kendler has worked with a sample of 28,616 twins from the Virginia general population registry. While this is not a formal representative sample, assuming twinning to be approximately random across demographic categories, the result should be a reasonably unbiased sample of Virginians. Interested in the effect of religion as a potential buffer against mental illness, Kendler and his associates selected 78 religiosity items from a variety of published questionnaires of religiosity and administered them to their twin sample. Most of the items ask Likert scale questions about their beliefs, for example, rating oneself on a five-point scale from "very religious" to "not at all religious." The problem with such ratings, discussed earlier, is that there is no way of knowing what "very" or "not at all" is to be compared to—other people, cultural definitions, and so on. However six items were found that seemed to use scales that had more definite anchor points; for example, "I feel God's presence: Many times a day, Every day, Most days, Some days, Once in while, Never or almost never." The results for the six items are presented in table 7.5. The responses have been categorized into five categories of religiosity. Averaging over the relevant responses, it appears that approximately 13 percent of the Virginia sample are devoted Christians, 22 percent are regular participants in Christian practice and belief, 20 percent are occasional participants, 35 percent are intermittent participants, and 15 percent are non-participants. These numbers are fairly close to the national results estimated by Morris Fiorina, based on a number of national surveys of church attendance. The results he reports are as follows: 16 percent never attend, 30 percent attend a few times a year, 16 percent once or twice a month, and 38 percent every week or almost every week. Interestingly, Fiorina finds a small decrease in overall attendance from 1980 to 2000 (Fiorina et al. 2005).

Another assessment of how important religious compared to nonreligious values are to Americans can be derived from Rokeach's

Table 7.5 Religiosity: Virginia sample

Question	Devoted Participation	Regular Participation	Occasional Participation	Intermittant Participation	Not Religious
I feel God's presence	Many times a day 10%	Every day 24%	Most days 19%	Some days or once in a while 32%	Never or almost never 15%
How often in the last year did you attend religious services	More than once a week 15%	Once a week 21%	A few times a month 14%	Less than once a month 29%	Never 16%
Other than at mealtime, I pray to God privately	Many times a day 14%	Every day 23%	Most days 20%	Some days or once in a while 32%	Never or almost never 11%
In general, how important are your religious or spiritual beliefs in your daily life?	Very important 51%			Somewhat important 34%	Not very or not at all important 15%
Have you been "born again," that is, had a turning point in your life when you committed yourself to Jesus?	Yes 54%			No 46%	
Please tell me whether you agree or disagree with the following statement: "The Bible is the actual world of God and is to be taken literally, word by word."	Agree 42%			Disagree 58%	
Rounded estimate for each column category	13%	22%	20%	35%	15%

Source: Data from Kendler et al. 2003.

representative samples of Americans, questioned in 1968, 1971, and 1981. In all four time periods, "Salvation (being saved, eternal life)" had almost exactly a median ranking compared to the other terminal values. Higher than Salvation (in rank order) were Family Security, Freedom, Happiness, Self-Respect, Wisdom, and Equality. Lower were a Comfortable Life, a Sense of Accomplishment, True Friendship, National Security, Inner Harmony, Mature Love, a World of Beauty, Social Recognition, Pleasure, and an Exciting Life (Rokeach and Ball-Rokeach 1989). When broken down by denomination, all the religious denominations except the Baptists gave Salvation a lower than median rank; for the Baptists Salvation was ranked third, behind A World at Peace and Family Security. Thus, while religion appears to be of moderate importance to a great majority of Americans, and of great importance to over a tenth, it tends not to be for most people an overriding value in the way security, freedom, and happiness are. However, the religious items have greater standard deviations than any other cluster. Americans vary greatly with respect to religiosity, and, as we shall see later, religion seems to work to create strong collectivist values.

Demographics

Another dashed expectation was the notion that different demographic categories would display strong and interesting differences in values. However, only small differences were found between American males and females, young and old, and rich and poor. With respect to male-female differences, only 4 of 58 cluster averages showed a significant difference of more than 0.2 standard deviations. Men value *understanding science*, *having social status*, and *enjoying comic, board games*, and *sports* slightly more than women do. Women value *being sexually restrained* slightly more than men. Overall, there is a tendency for women to value *altruism* more than men. Age differences were negligible. Standard SES differences were small, although there was clear trend for high ratings of *individualism* to increase as SES increased. The difference between SES level I and SES level V was less than half a standard deviation.

In the social science world, the three major variables are age, gender, and SES—major in the sense that many human characteristics show important differences across these three variables. However, this is not what was found. The largest value differences were related to religion. Figure 7.4 shows a plot for the average *individualism* and *altruism* scores for gender, SES, and religion. Traditional categories—for

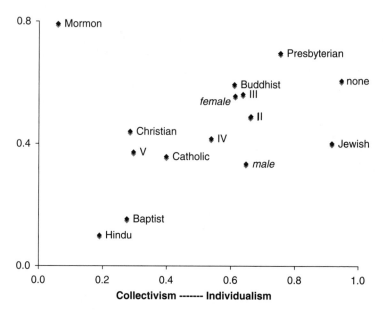

Figure 7.4 American Sample: gender, SES, and religion by *individualism/ collectivism* and *altruism/self-interest*.

example, Episcopalian—with less than three respondents were not included. The chart shows graphically the spread of the wider spread of religious groups compared to gender or SES.

A fairly large percentage of respondents used the term "Christian" to designate their religious denomination. Although the term is ambiguous, the value coordinates of Christians in figure 7.4 indicate that this group is probably composed primarily of respondents who think of themselves as born-again Christians. Across religious groups there is a full standard deviation spread on the *individualism* dimension, with Mormons, Hindus, Christians, and Baptists displaying more collectivist values, while Jews, Presbyterians, and those with no religious affiliation displaying more individualistic orientations. These results are similar to the results found by Rokeach. To dimensionalize Rokeach's data (Rokeach 1969), a correspondence analysis was carried out of the value rankings for religious groups after double normalizing; that is, normalizing both the rows and columns of the rank order matrix (Weller and Romney 1990). The first dimension for the Rokeach data is clearly interpretable as *individualism* versus *collectivism*. None of the other dimensions were interpretable. The results are presented in figure 7.5.

Individualism vs collectivism	Loading
Independent	0.64
Intellectual	0.63
An exciting life	0.60
Inner harmony	0.54
Mature love	0.54
Nonbeliever (45)	0.54
Episcopalian (39)	0.51
Jewish (28)	0.49
Imaginative	0.49
A sense of accomplishment	0.47
Logical	0.46
Capable	0.39
Broadminded	0.36
Family security	0.33
Responsible	0.33
Self controlled	0.28
Presbyterian (76)	0.18
Wisdom	0.18
True friendship	0.15
Pleasure	0.09
Equality	0.08
Social recognition	0.02
Loving	−0.02
Congregationalist (39)	−0.04
Freedom	−0.12
Honest	−0.15
A comfortable life	−0.17
Happiness	−0.18
National security	−0.22
Courageous	−0.22
Helpful	−0.25
Lutheran (113)	−0.31
A world of beauty	−0.32
Catholic (322)	−0.38
Self-respect	−0.41
Cheerful	−0.45
Polite	−0.45
Methodist (199)	−0.48
Baptist (324)	−0.51
Salvation	−0.54
Ambitious	−0.60
Forgiving	−0.61
Clean	−0.62
A world at peace	−0.63
Obedient	−0.64

Figure 7.5 Correspondence analysis of Rokeach values by religion.

Both the Three Society data and the Rokeach data suggest that religion has a direct effect on values. This effect might come about because the different denominations form moral communities in which different values are taught and practiced. The values of a religious group are a part of belonging to that community, and likely to be under normative pressure. Gender, on the other hand, is not usually the basis of a moral community, although in cases of ideologically committed feminist groups, for example, or road warriors, one would expect to find strong communally influenced values. It may be that specific occupations also have communally based value orientations. Rokeach, for example, found that scientists and police officers have relatively distinctive value profiles, the police rating *being self-controlled* and *being logical* higher than the average American, scientists rating *being intellectual, being imaginative,* and *a sense of accomplishment* higher than the average American (Rokeach et al. 1971, Rokeach 1979).

Chapter 8

The Vietnamese

The Vietnamese sample is composed of immigrants living in California and North Carolina. The two separate geographical regions were chosen because the experience of Vietnamese in southern California may be atypical for Vietnamese immigrants, many of whom do not live in communities in which many of their neighbors are also Vietnamese. In this chapter, both quantitative and qualitative ethnographic materials are presented. The integration of these different kinds of data is carried out by describing actual life problems and decisions faced by families and individuals, attempting to show how values enter into what happens and how what happens is understood and reacted to. One of the points that emerges is that values are related in complex ways to both the cultural world and to individual motivations. For example, among the Vietnamese, strong values and motivations to succeed are blended with a collectivist orientation to form what is called the *family-based achievement syndrome* (Caplan et al. 1991). Issues concerning family success can overcome strong individual achievement wishes, creating internal conflict but also a strong and valued family world.

As part of the research project, packets containing a personality questionnaire, a cultural values questionnaire, and a demographic questionnaire were distributed to respondents in their homes and at public meeting places. Participants were asked to fill out the questionnaires at home during the next week and these were retrieved from participants after completion. Most were relatively recent arrivals: 89 percent left Vietnam in 1979 or later. The average time a respondent had been in the United States was 11 years. Of the 233 respondents, 119 were female, 114 male. Fifty-seven respondents were living in North Carolina, 176 in California. The age range was 17–88 with a mean of 39.7. First-wave immigrants (those fleeing Vietnam in 1975) tended to be part of the urban, intellectual elite. Post-1979 immigrants tend to be from more rural, lower-SES backgrounds. In general, these later immigrants face greater difficulty in acclimating to the United States, due in part to the "compassion fatigue" of the

United States and in part to shifts in the U.S. economy (Freeman 1995). Twenty percent of informants' household incomes fell in the range of $30,000–$49,000 total annual household income—this was the overall modal income category. While the percentage of households below the poverty line was not small—30.1 percent reported incomes of $19,000 or below—26 percent of the respondents reported annual household incomes over $50,000. Numerous components are at play here—households have multiple income sources, and income levels tend to rise steadily with time spent in the United States. In addition to administering the personality inventory, ethnographic research included living with two Vietnamese-American families, conducting participant observation of a number of families throughout their day, and conducting in-depth interviews with a broad range of Vietnamese Americans.

California and North Carolina represent two distinct sociocultural environments for immigrants in the United States: one a region with bustling ethnic enclaves, the other a region with a relatively scarce Asian- or Vietnamese-American population. The San Diego area has scores of Vietnamese restaurants, groceries, and other businesses and lies within easy driving distance of Westminster, California's Little Saigon, the neighborhood widely considered the capital of Vietnamese America. With its bountiful immigrant population, thriving ethnic businesses, and several Vietnamese-language newspapers, modern San Diego resembles eastern cities of the late-nineteenth and early twentieth centuries where immigrant groups carved out zones of social and cultural autonomy within the larger fabric of American life (Leininger 2001).

Not all Vietnamese immigrants to the United States moved to cities or regions with well-established or numerically dense Vietnamese-American communities. Initially, U.S. policy was to spread Vietnamese refugee resettlement equally across the 50 states in hopes of avoiding greater economic impact on any one state or region. The concentration of Vietnamese Americans in California (45.6 percent of Vietnamese Americans live in California, according to the 1990 census) is a result of voluntary secondary migration. Smaller, yet sizable, Vietnamese populations continue to exist, though, across the United States. Raleigh, North Carolina, like its sister cities, Greensboro and Charlotte, is one such metropolitan area containing a small Vietnamese-American population. Although it supports a handful of Vietnamese-owned businesses and stages large annual Tet celebrations, Raleigh's Vietnamese-American population remains scattered across the city rather than clustered in ethnic enclaves.

Despite these differences in geography and population density, Vietnamese-American family life in both San Diego and Raleigh resembles the patterns of family life described in earlier studies of Vietnamese Americans (Leininger 2001). In both regions, education is highly valued and family obligations play a central role in educational pursuits (Caplan et al. 1989, Zhou and Bankston 1994). Vietnamese-American families across the country are also characterized by important differences in experiences of first-generation, 1.5-generation, and second-generation family members (Rumbaut 1991, Zhou and Bankston 1998), and the difficulties encountered by individuals and families as a result of these generational differences (Freeman 1989, Kibria 1993)—that is, of differences in acculturation level resulting from age at the time of immigration. In Vietnamese-American families in both regions, it is also typical for first-generation parents to have experienced post-migration downward mobility and for this trend to be in the process of being reversed by the high frequency of 1.5-generation Vietnamese Americans who earn engineering, DDS, PharmD, and MD degrees.

The 328-item questionnaire was translated with the assistance of bilingual research informants into Vietnamese using standard back-translation techniques (Werner and Campbell 1970). Translators were all Vietnamese Americans who had been born in and attended school in Vietnam and whose first language was Vietnamese, and who were attending college in the United States. Groups of two or three made an initial translation and then a different translator would provide a backtranslation. Items for which backtranslations indicated difficulties were discussed and revised until a more satisfactory translation was found.

Respondents were instructed to *Danh dau tam quan trong cua moi cau sau doi voi ban* (mark the importance of each phrase according to you), from 0, *Khong quan trong* (not important), to 4, *Rat quan trong* (very important). The questionnaire was distributed through community contacts and local advertisements. Respondents were also given a Vietnamese translation of the NEO personality questionnaire (Leininger 2001) making possible an analysis of relations between values and personality characteristics.

In table 7.2 in chapter 7, we saw that the top 10 Vietnamese items contrast strongly with the top American items. For the Vietnamese, the highest of the 328 items is *having deep respect for parents and grandparents*. The second highest item is *taking care of my parents when they get older. Not dishonoring my family, fulfilling family obligations,* and *not dishonoring my family* are also among the top 10 items. Employment issues are also prominent, including the items *being employed* and *having a secure job.* We shall see later in the analysis that these two values are linked together in a culturally institutionalized syndrome called *family-based achievement.* The Vietnamese top items also display a moral emphasis exemplified by the *items treating human life as precious, following my conscience and doing right,* and *being responsible.*

Figure 8.1 shows the differences between the Vietnamese and the Three Society average. As indicated by the top 10 items, the Vietnamese are less *individualistic* and more *collectivistic* than the other two societies. However, there are almost no significant differences between the Vietnamese and the average society for the *altruism* dimension or the *industry* dimension.

A central feature of communalistic societies is the individual's relation to the group. The Vietnamese correlations of the other value items with the specific item *going along with the group,* in contrast to the American correlations for the same item, show a distinct pattern. The data are presented in table 8.1.

Both societies show clear linkages of *going along with group decisions* to tradition—for the Americans *maintaining old traditions* and *having strong traditions,* for the Vietnamese *taking part in ceremonies, being religious, and observing religious holidays.* Both also have linkages with items relating to social solidarity; for the Americans *feeling that one belongs* and *being part of a group,* for the Vietnamese *being with people who feel about things the way I do, having trust in others,* and so on. But there are also strong contrasts between the two societies; the Vietnamese link *going along with group decisions* with creative planning *(thinking ahead, being open to new ideas, thinking up new ways of doing things)* while the American associations are with what might be called constricted conformity *(fitting in, respecting authority, being obedient, not standing out from others, etc.).* Apparently, for the Vietnamese, *going along with group decisions* does not mean one does not express oneself—on the contrary, group decisions are associated with creativity and openness. Creativity and openness are normally considered individualistic values, but for the Vietnamese these items are associated with group process. Finally, the Americans associate *going along with group decisions* with wealth and status; perhaps the idea here is that wealth and status involve conformity to group norms.

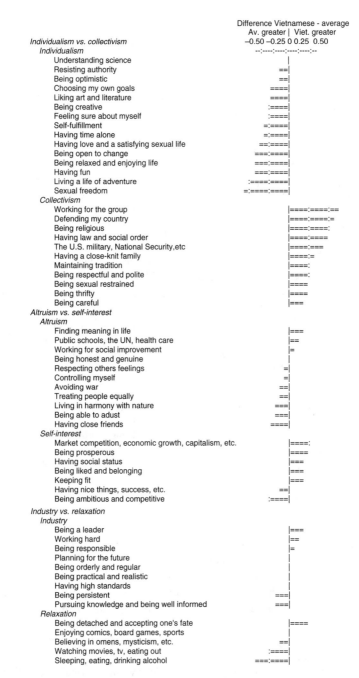

Figure 8.1 Comparison of Vietnamese to Three Society average on 58 cluster.

Table 8.1 Top twenty correlations with *going along with group decisions*

r	Vietnamese	r	Americans
0.24	Cooperating with others	0.24	Feeling that one belongs
0.19	Being with people who feel about things the way I do	0.24	Being part of a group
0.19	Having trust in others	0.21	Having others think well of me
0.17	Keeping in touch with old friends	0.20	Having a well-organized society
0.14	Taking part in ceremonies	0.19	Maintaining old traditions
0.18	Being religious	0.19	Having strong traditions
0.18	Observing religious holidays		
0.16	Having a well-organized society	0.36	Fitting in
		0.25	Respecting authority
0.18	Being open to new ideas	0.22	Being obedient
0.17	Thinking ahead	0.22	Not standing out from others
0.17	Thinking up new ways of doing things	0.20	Being reserved and acting with discretion
0.27	Completing work on time	0.19	Taking the viewpoint of others
0.18	Keeping things tidy		
0.16	Having financial security	0.25	Being well dressed
		0.27	Having great wealth
0.14	Being patient and resigned when misfortunes occur	0.23	Having a secure job
0.21	Coming to terms with the shortness of life	0.22	Having a leisurely lifestyle
0.15	Being able to adjust	0.20	Making good a profit
0.14	Having emotional ties with the natural environment	0.21	Having good looks
		0.19	Being approved of
0.16	Having a leisurely lifestyle	0.19	Being the center of attention
0.18	Depreciating myself and complimenting others		

Another of the 328 items that shows interesting differences between Vietnamese and Americans is *finding meaning in life*. The top correlations for *finding meaning in life* are presented in table 8.2.

For the both the Vietnamese and the Americans, *finding meaning in life* is linked to personal integrity—*being true to oneself*. For the Vietnamese, *finding meaning in life* is also related to *a positive outlook on life* and *being optimistic*. For Americans there are linkages to *seeking universal truths* and *coming to terms with the shortness of life*. Both societies have linkages to benevolent values—for the Americans,

Table 8.2   Top twenty correlations with *finding meaning in life*

r	Vietnamese	r	Americans
0.47	Being true to myself	0.25	Being honest and genuine
0.20	Having my own point of view	0.23	Understanding myself
0.17	Feeling sure about myself	0.21	Not deceiving others
0.23	Thinking about the future	0.16	Being true to myself
0.23	Having a positive outlook on life	0.34	Seeking universal truths
0.23	Not giving up	0.22	Coming to terms with the shortness of life
0.20	Being optimistic	0.19	Gaining experience and wisdom from suffering
0.18	Having a leisurely lifestyle	0.20	Feeling the pain of others
0.17	Being relaxed	0.20	Forgiving others
0.17	Having time to relax and take it easy	0.19	Understanding people who think differently
0.24	Maintaining equal opportunity for all	0.26	Having a world free of war
0.22	Understanding people who think differently	0.24	Treating human life as precious
0.19	Treating people equally	0.24	Not having social distinctions between people
0.18	Following my conscience and doing right	0.21	Avoiding war
		0.19	Increasing welfare for the disadvantaged
0.26	Being reliable	0.16	Battling for a cause
0.21	Being polite and well mannered	0.22	Finding a mate with good moral and intellectual qualities
0.17	Having others think well of me		

having a world free of war, treating human life as precious, and so on, for the Vietnamese *maintaining equal opportunity for all, treating people equally*, and so on. With respect to interpersonal behavior the Vietnamese correlations with *finding meaning in life* are with *being reliable, polite, and well thought of*, while the Americans' correlations are with *feeling the pain of others* and *forgiving others*. The overall tone for the Americans seems grimmer and more moralistic than that of the Vietnamese, who give a greater emphasis to optimism and leisure as part of the search for meaning. Here it appears we see reflexes of the contrast between the Judeo-Christian ethic and a Buddhist-Confucian ethic.

Family-Based Achievement

One of the central characteristic thought to distinguish Vietnamese American from nonimmigrant U.S. American families, and to play a major role in Vietnamese-American families' rapid socioeconomic and educational improvements and successes over the last decades, is the presence of a syndrome that has been called *family-based achievement* (Caplan et al. 1991, p. 80). As a value orientation this syndrome emphasizes the family as a central institution through which achievement and knowledge are accomplished. There is a strong collective obligation among family members, plus the subordination of individual needs to the needs of the larger family unit. This value orientation is thought to be compatible with U.S. American values because of its emphasis on the values of hard work and achievement so central to the Protestant Ethic, but culturally distinctive in its emphasis on the family as means and end of work and achievement. Caplan et al. (1991), in a principal components analysis of Indochinese refugees' value ratings, found a component that they titled *family-based achievement* marked by a concern for education, achievement, respect for family members, and family loyalty.

The Vietnamese top correlations with *having a close-knit family* presented in table 8.3 provide further evidence for the importance of the *family-based achievement syndrome*. The Vietnamese correlations include not only items dealing with the family *(having deep respect for parents and grandparents, having a raising children,* etc.), but also a distinct cluster of items dealing with work and responsibility *(having a secure job, being thrifty, being responsible,* etc.). The contrasting American correlations show no connections to employment or responsibility, although the actual ratings of Americans on these items are as high as the Vietnamese ratings.

Further evidence for the *family-based achievement* syndrome comes from a study in which Vietnamese Americans rated their personal beliefs about the characteristics of their own and other ethnic groups by Burton, Greenberger, and Hayward (2005). Correspondence analysis of their data yielded a first dimension on which Vietnamese Americans are perceived as possessing a cluster of traits including "hardworking," "reliable," "stingy," and "family-oriented." Burton and colleagues refer to this cluster of traits as the *Collectivist Achievement Ethic*, noting that it shares with the Protestant Ethic traits related to hard work, but reflects a collectivist version of the

Table 8.3 Top twenty correlations with *having a closeknit family*

r	Vietnamese	r	Americans
0.43	Having deep respect for parents and grandparents	0.65	Being close to my family
0.38	Having and raising children	0.49	Fulfilling family obligations
0.34	Finding a mate with good moral and intellectual qualities	0.49	Having big family gatherings
0.33	Preserving the family name	0.48	Having deep respect for parents and grandparents
0.32	Being close to my family	0.43	Taking care of my parents when they get older
0.31	Fulfilling family obligations	0.37	Marrying someone my parents would approve of
0.27	Having big family gatherings	0.36	Not dishonoring my family
0.27	Taking care of my parents when they get older	0.32	Having and raising children
0.26	Not dishonoring my family	0.32	Not getting divorced
		0.29	Preserving the family name
0.38	Being persistent	0.22	Getting along with my spouse's family and friends
0.34	Having a secure job	0.28	Taking responsibility for my siblings
0.31	Being thrifty		
0.25	Being employed		
0.24	Working hard	0.23	Being sexually modest
0.24	Taking responsibility for decisions	0.24	Having strong traditions
		0.19	Showing respect to older people
0.29	Being responsible		
0.30	Having close supportive friends	0.28	Having love
0.26	Promoting Vietnamese cultural values	0.22	Being pleasant
		0.21	Being relaxed
0.26	Being healthy	0.19	Not giving up
0.25	My country		
0.32	National heath care		

Protestant Ethic, in which "accomplishment is oriented toward the needs and goals of the group, including the family."

Ethnographic Materials

During the period between 1997 and 2000, Leininger carried out ethnographic field work among Vietnamese. The addition of the results from qualitative ethnographic research to the Vietnamese data gives a richer assessment of the place of values in respondents' lives than survey research alone. In her ethnographic research Leininger found that collectivist values contribute to Vietnamese Americans' adaptation to American life not just by motivating them to engage in practices that lead to educational and occupational success, but also by influencing them not to select possible life trajectories that would threaten the continued socioeconomic viability of the family.

For example, the actions of Bac Khanh, a close informant, appear to be reflections of collectivist values and the *family-based achievement* syndrome. Bác Khanh reasoned that in order for her children to be successful in school, they need time to study. Therefore, she delegated to herself the task of doing everything that needed to be done for her children, preparing and serving them meals and doing their laundry in addition to her full-time work at a restaurant that she and a relative co-owned. She put in 16-hour days and saw her long hours not only as a way of taking care of her children, but also as a practical pursuit of the quickest route to family success: ensuring the success of her children.

Bác Khanh's devoted work as both breadwinner and housewife also meant that she abandoned all hope of returning to her former career as a pharmacist. Instead, Bác Khanh took business classes at the local community college in hopes of gaining skills that would help her in her restaurant. In this regard, her work serves as an example of collectivism taking precedence over individualism. Her goals appear selfless in contrast to the typical U.S. motivation for having a career. The point of her work is not that it is individualistically satisfying. Rather, for her, the value of her works is that it provides an income with which to support one's family. As Bác Khanh put it:

> [For Vietnamese women], anything make money for family okay. You see a lot. The Vietnamese women. And I am too. In my country I have to study the high level, but I come here I make anything [to] get money for my family. For my children. I don't care.... I can get a job lower or anything I make money. I think that better. Make life better. Because in my country I have the big house, I have the [servants] help me. But come here I do anything.

Bác Khanh regretted that her poor English and lack of an American degree prevented her from continuing in her chosen career in the United States. But for Vietnamese women like her, work that provides for one's family—satisfying family collectivistic values—makes it highly motivating.

Perhaps the strongest evidence for the strength of family collectivism values among first-generation Vietnamese American women comes from conversations with women like Bác Khanh about their dissatisfaction with their marriages and their resolution to stay in their marriages for the sake of their children. Leininger's interviews with Bác Khanh are filled with direct, negative evaluations of the unfairnesses of the Vietnamese patriarchal norms in general and of her own husband and marriage in particular. Bác Khanh often expressed direct criticisms of her husband (Bác Phuùc's), as in the following interview segment in which she complains about his unwillingness to help more with household chores and his squandering of time and money by going out with his friends.

> BÁC KHANH: I don't like Bác Phuùc's hobby. Because he like to visit around. Weekend go out, visit around. Friend or um—I think once a month is better. But once a week, too much. He don't like to clean up my house or anything. He go around.
>
> AL: Mmhmm. [pause] He doesn't help you clean.
>
> BÁC KHANH: Weekends I wash their clothes and I clean up my house. But sometimes I don't have time! Because Saturday I work until 2:00 and I go to the store and I get home at 4 or 5, I prepare for dinner. After that I very tired. I can't clean. And then Sunday I go to the laundry room. Wash my clothes and Nga's and Tân's clothes and Bác Phuùc. Sometimes I don't have time clean up my house. And in the week I go to school and I have work and cooking everything.
>
> AL: Yeah. Very busy. [pause] Do you ask Bác Phuùc to help you clean?
>
> BÁC KHANH: I ask—a lot! But—
>
> AL: He doesn't—
>
> BÁC KHANH: You living with me about two months. You see! You see! Before I have to go to school, I cooking. I cooking. I go to work and go to school every day. Sometime Nga told him, "Daddy! You unfair!" [laughs] Bác Phuùc—simple for the man in family—like that in my country a lot. Women the generation same as Nga in the U.S. I think better than in my country. Because my country the man in the family have powerful. And like a king. Because my country call husband is king, wife is slave.

Despite her dissatisfaction with Bác Phúc's failure to help, Bác Khanh continued to put in 16-hour days, supporting the family both financially and with her own direct labor. Her *family-based achievement* orientation and her *collectivist* family values manifested themselves in the overriding of her individual wish for a more fair division of labor in her family and in her steady contribution of 16-hour days to the family in spite of her discontent. While it cannot be demonstrated that her collectivistic family values are the major motive for her long hours and careful family planning, it can be shown quite directly that she valorizes the work she does by referring to these collectivistic family values.

The severity of Bác Khanh's dissatisfaction with her marriage became apparent in a later interview when she revealed that her husband had been unfaithful to her, and that she had thought about divorce but had decided not to divorce for her children's (Nga's and Tân's) sake.

> BÁC KHANH: …My feelings were hurt very much. [pause] At that time I decide to divorce but I thinking about Nga and Tân.
> AL: Yeah.
> BÁC KHANH: I ah, I would like Nga graduate. I will go anywhere with Nga. Where Nga get a job, a good job, I will go with Nga. Because right now I need to study English more. After that I will [laughs] go to work and when Nga [inaud]…

Like most Vietnamese-American women, Bác Khanh feared that divorcing her husband would make her children unmarriageable. She, therefore, resolved to stay with her husband, in spite of her wish to divorce him, in order to ensure the well-being of her children. Her internalized collectivist family values, then, had consequences in Bác Khanh's life beyond committing her to hard labor. Living according to these values was indeed intrinsically taxing because she was performing the majority of the family's housework in addition to working full time. But further, following these values necessitated Bác Khanh's abandonment of her chosen career in pharmacy and led her to endure an unfair and hurtful marriage she would have liked to end.

Collectivist family values have a similarly complex relationship to the lives of first-generation Vietnamese-American husband-fathers. Collectivist family values are displayed in family decisions to leave Vietnam and endure a status loss in the United States for the sake of their children. For example, Bác Leã, like many Vietnamese-American men Leininger became acquainted with, cited his children as his primary reason for coming to the United States. After his release from the Communist prison, Bác Leã was determined to move his family out of Vietnam because Communist policy discriminated against the children of former South Vietnamese officers, making it highly unlikely that they would be admitted to institutions of higher education. He successfully escaped, spent six months in a refugee camp, and eventually was allowed to resettle in the United States. His wife and children joined him later. Once in the United States, Bác Leã got a two-year degree that enabled him to find wage work as an electrician. His work as an electrician was not only an immense decrease in status from his previous status as a high-ranking South Vietnamese army officer, but it was also monotonous and unenjoyable. Bác Leã often complained that he was "so tired" and that had he stayed in Vietnam, he would have retired by now. But he also made it clear that it was important to him to work now to help secure his children's future, and that he did not regret having come to the United States. Leininger observed: "While talking about the hardships of escaping from Vietnam and coming to San Diego and finding work, Bác Leã suddenly points to Tân [his son, who is sitting nearby watching TV] and says, 'and I have to leave, I have no choice, because I am so worried about this one, this little guy. Because he won't get a good education in Vietnam.'"

While they are committed to their families and children, first-generation Vietnamese-American men struggle with a painful and often shameful loss of social and socioeconomic status entailed by their immigration. Another informant, Bác Tam, spent several years studying English and attempting to find a position as a professor of biology, his former profession in Vietnam. Nothing worked out, though, and eventually attended a community college to become an accountant. He experienced great shame at entering what he considered such a lowly position. Evidence for this comes from the several times he referred to himself as a *cu li* (coolie; unskilled, lowly laborer) as in the following interview excerpt: "I have two lives. One is a *cu li*, an American accountant and another one is Vietnamese national professor of biology. I will be free to choose after Cân graduates."

Bác Tam felt not only that he had lost his authority in the family, but that this loss of authority coincided with being deprived of his children's loving adoration. He expresses this feeling of deprivation in the following interview segment. When the segment begins, Bác Tâm has been talking about his willingness to die for his parents—a topic, which he initiated, that served as a thought experiment exploring some of the logical consequences of collectivist family values.

> BÁC TÂM: I can die for my parents. And I am going to die for my sons or daughter *if* in the condition—*if* they love me. They respect me and they love me I am going to die for them but if they do not respect me or they don't love me, I won't die for them.
>
> AL: Mmhmm.
>
> BÁC TÂM: I don't have many people in life to die for. To risk my life for. [pause] If Cân, Hieáu, and Phöõïng love me—and respect me and they stick to me, close to me in a likable or—treating me in a tender manner and I feel, I can feel they love me, I am going to die for them. For example when they are young, they always sit or play around me, even when I sleep they lie on my chest, on my back and doze off on my chest, on my back. And each time I say something to them that is

proof, there is no negotiation. So [at] that time if they are in danger I am going to die for them. Not now. Not now, they—seem they are superior to me in knowledge in American culture. They think I have to adjust to the new culture. But my adjustment is not as good as theirs. So they don't respect me any more. They try to challenge me about knowledge, about education. They think that they know more than me in American culture and American education. And they do not respect me anymore. Through our conversation I feel that.

AL: Through your conversation with your children?

BÁC TÂM: [nods yes]. So I don't risk my life for them. But I will when they were young and relied on me completely. Everything I say is the truth. What I did is the right thing to do.

AL: Mmhmm.

BÁC TÂM: They loved me because I took good care of them. I feed them to the age of nine I still feed them. And when they go to school, when they just got the driver license I stay next to them when they were driving and then they go to their class and I slept in the car. For four or five hours. [pause] But when I walk with them around the NCSU campus, they try to evade me. They feel embarrassed or something.

AL: Mmmm.

BÁC TÂM: At that age they want to separate from me. I used to wait for them two or three hours, nothing happen. But if Cân or Hieáu or Phööïng were coming and I was a little late for half an hour they make faces. They make face. And they get angry, "Why you didn't come on time?!" Make them waiting! It's not fair. So right now [laughs] I won't risk my life for them.

In this interview excerpt, Bác Tâm expresses how hurt he feels at his children's lack of devotion by asserting that he is no longer willing to risk his life for them as he was when they showed him love and respect. But despite Bác Tâm's disappointment and sadness about his loss of his authority and of his children's love, he remained dedicated to them. For example, when Bác Tâm's son Phööïng got married to someone Bác Tâm disapproved of, Bác Tâm was angry, to be sure, but continued to make sacrifices for Phööïng—buying him a car and paying off his college loans, for example. Sacrifices such as these revealed that Bác Tam's obligation to his children was not extinguished by his sadness and disappointment at their failure to love and fulfill their obligations to him.

Bác Tam and Bác Leã both planned to eventually return permanently to Vietnam. These plans helped fight their loss of a sense of themselves as being efficacious, intelligent, respected, beneficent, and useful. That they were in fact being efficacious and useful by being present in their children's lives and by swallowing their pride and taking on "lowly" careers in order to provide for their children and families was not sufficient to combat the shame of being a *cu li* or the pain of having lost their children's respect and devoted love. In their minds, only returning to their lives in Vietnam would assuage the humiliation and deprivation. But their value-informed strong sense of obligation to provide for and protect their children until they received their degrees and were married held them from immediately leaving the United States. They deferred their plans to return to Vietnam, looking forward to being free to do so after their children finished school and became self-sufficient.

Relations of Values to Motivation and Behavior

The integration of qualitative and quantitative analyses in this chapter produces a picture of the importance of the *family-based achievement* syndrome, which has been such an important part of the Vietnamese success in the United States. Caplan et al. find the Vietnamese predisposition to success to be cultural compatibility. Refugees brought with them Buddhist and Confucian values that have motivated and guided them toward a successful course in American life (Caplan et al. 1991, p. 139).

It is important to note that these values are being enacted in daily practices, such as devoting evening hours to homework, telling stories and reading to the children, and the cooperative pooling of resources in employment and education (Caplan et al. 1991, pp. 139–140, Leininger 2001). In these practices, cultural values are "connect[ed] to the living present through the development of strategies to survive, to get ahead, guided by the ethical and practical doctrines embedded in the culture" (p. 140). Caplan et al. point out that an educationally successful family depends on its effectiveness on a set of family norms based on cultural values that make for a lifestyle that helps the Vietnamese face adversity and prepares them for success (p. 141).

The values that go into the family-based achievement syndrome are strongly internalized: they act as life motivations. Bác Tam strongly feels he should stay in the United States and to do what he can to provide for his family; Bác Khanh feels she should stay in her marriage and continue working extremely long hours every day. In both cases, collectivist family values impact action by means of the strong sense of *shouldness* they evoke. And this *shouldness* is not just an internal sense; the values on family are built into the norms for family roles. That is, the *shouldness* is normative, it is a socially agreed upon way that mothers and fathers should act, and which is sanctioned by disapproval if they do not do as they should. Such standard, expected, normative actions are called *cultural practices*.

It should also be noted that values are just one part of the psycho-dynamic equation. First, *shoulds* often stand in conflict with other desires that people have. Vietnamese values do a great deal of work in keeping in place the family social system by warding off wishes that threaten the family. If Bác Khanh were to act on her wish to divorce her husband, or if Bác Tam were to act on his wish to return to Vietnam, their family as a collective would no longer exist. Vietnamese collective values contribute to a system in which individuals are moti-vated to behave in ways that will benefit the family. These values contribute to family-based achievement not merely by providing a blueprint of what should be done, and not only by providing the felt motivation of *shouldness*, but also by motivating family members to abandon other wishes that might interfere with *family-based achieve-ment*. To enact the practices that bring about deeply internalized val-ues, is gratifying for individuals in that it creates the social entity, the family, which in turn provides for them. Also, pursuing and achieving goals that are linked to deeply internalized values can be a source of gratification. At the same time, though, the pursuit of these goals often results in the frustration of other desires and demands that other desires be abandoned. The dynamic between values and motivations—at time conjoint and fused, at time opposed or leading in different directions—is a central fact of human existence. More facets of this issue are discussed in the chapters that follow.

Demographics

Figure 8.2 presents a chart of the positions by gender, generation, religion, and area of the country on the individualism and altruism dimensions. The gender differences are small, with females on the average only one-seventh of a standard deviation more *collectivistic* than the males. The specific item showing the largest difference is *being sexually restrained* (females 0.4, males 0.1). The differences between the North Carolina and California samples are of about the same size, with the California sample showing the stronger collectiv-istic values. The differences by generation and religion are somewhat larger, with a difference of approximately one-fourth of a standard deviation between the 1.0 generation (those who arrived in the United States as adults) and the later 1.5 generation (those who arrived as

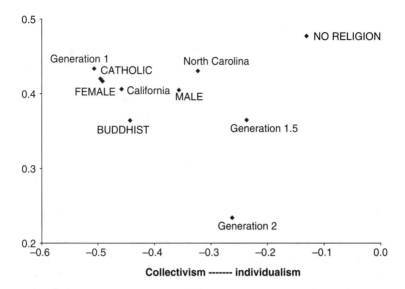

Figure 8.2 Vietnamese sample: gender, religion, and generation by *individualism/collectivism* and *altrusim/self-interest*.

preadolescents) and 2.0 generation (those born in the United States. The 2.0 generation is less benevolent than either of the earlier generations, with higher ratings for *having social status* and *being ambitious and competitive*. The largest differences are found with respect to religion, with those saying they have no religion being more individualistic by almost half a standard deviation. There are no especially marked specific items; rather there is a general tendency for all collectivism and individualism items to be affected. As in the American data, the effect of demographic variables is small. Where there are differences they appear to be the result of inhabiting slightly different moral communities than differences due to the effect of individual life experiences.

Values and Personality

A personality questionnaire was also included as part of Leininger's Vietnamese research. The personality test used was the International Personality Item Pool (IPIP) version of the NEO-PI-R (Goldberg 1999) and is described in Leininger (2002). The NEO has been administered to samples from a number of different societies, and shows good similarity in structure and translatability. In the NEO questionnaire, respondents are asked to rate how accurately each item describes them. The English items are brief verbal phrases, for example, "lose my temper," "seldom get lost in thought," "look at the bright side of life." The Vietnamese translation adds the pronoun *toi* ("I") to each item. Respondents rated themselves on a five-point scale, from 1 (very inaccurate) to 5 (very accurate). The Goldberg's administration of the NEO-IPIP to a sample in Oregon has been used as the American comparison.

The same backtranslation methods described earlier were used to produce the Vietnamese NEO, and involved some interesting problems. For example, one of the items on the *trust* scale, "believe people are basically moral" backtranslated as, "even though people sometimes do something bad, I believe everyone has morals." Although the translation seemed roughly accurate, in fact the translators appeared not to fully understand the meaning of the item in either its English or Vietnamese version, suggesting that this item is too culturally specific. On the whole, the average alpha mean of 0.70 and the expected five-component structure, discussed later, suggest that the translation was successful, albeit with room for improvement.

While not planned in the original research design, the opportunity to relate the values dimensions to the NEO dimensions permits an important investigation of the relation between values and personality. David McClelland (1951) divided personality into three different sets of variables. The first set of variables consists of character *traits*; traits are general tendencies in a person's responses, such as being outgoing, or being depressed. McClelland referred to the second set of personality variables as *basic cognitive schemas*, such as the general conception that people can be trusted, or that hard work will be rewarded. A person may be more or less aware of these schemas; a racist, for example, might be unaware of holding a racist schema. The third set of variables concerns *motivation*; the things a person wants and strives for. The motivations may be episodic or chronic, conscious or unconscious, general or specific. In McClelland's terms, the NEO consists of self-report judgments on personality *traits* (i.e., the degree to which someone is extroverted, agreeable, etc.). McClelland concluded that the self-attribution data is primarily about a person's attitudes or values. Respondents taking a questionnaire are faced with a self-descriptive statement—for example, "I like to work on hard problems." The answer to a question like this is influenced by the tendency to sincerely see oneself in a good light. Thus people who value achievement see themselves as working hard and having high standards of excellence. However, McClelland argued, a person telling a story is less aware of disclosing motivational information, and more personally revealing of less conscious internal states.

Whether the Thematic Apperception Test (TAT) is a good technique for measuring motives remains controversial. But McClelland is correct in saying that self-attribution data is strongly influenced by self-relevant values. For example, if one takes a group of respondents and asks them to rate themselves on trait adjectives, the results are affected by the degree to which the trait is considered good or bad. One demonstration of this is to take a sample of respondents and ask them to make semantic ratings of a series of trait terms with respect to goodness, then take a second sample of respondents and ask them to rate themselves on the same terms. Each individual's scores can then be correlated with trait evaluation scores. Typically, the correlations are in the 0.3 to 0.4 range. However, if individual scores are *averaged* to give a group profile, *the average scores will correlate above 0.95 with the semantic evaluation of these traits.* This happens because the goodness of a term acts as a constant effect on each individual's rating, while the idiosyncratic component of each person's scores is averaged out by the idiosyncratic components of the scores of other people. *The result is that the group profile is almost entirely a reflection of the rater's evaluation of the goodness of the traits.* This does not mean that self-report tests such as the NEO measure nothing but how highly people evaluate items, since any other constant effect will also show up in the averages. This phenomenon of group averages on self-reports being strongly influenced by values makes it important to investigate with different populations the relations between values and self-reported personality traits in order to discover whether there are really any differences between the two kinds of ratings.

Component Structure

The five-component structure of the NEO has been found in over 20 linguistically distinct societies (McCrae and Costa 1997b, McCrae et al. 1998). For the Vietnamese data a Procrustes rotation (McCrae et al. 1996) was performed to align the NEO-IPIP with the NEO-PI-R in the U.S. American data Results of this rotation yielded a close fit between the two structures: all component and item congruence scores are above 0.9, indicating that the NEO-IPIP replicates the structure found using the NEO-PI-R. All five components of the NEO are readily recognizable in the Procrustes rotation.

Perhaps it should not be surprising to find the degree of cross-cultural sharing for the NEO to be as great or greater than the sharing of values. The correlation between the American means for the 30 facets of the NEO and the Vietnamese facets is 0.91, in contrast to the correlation between value clusters for the American and Vietnamese of 0.53. The mean correlations among Vietnamese respondents is 0.34, approximately the same as the 0.32 correlation for the value data. Thus the degree of sharing *among* respondents is about the same for the values data and the NEO personality data, but the similarity between the means for the two societies are even greater for the NEO personality data than the values data. Bar graphs for the NEO facet means for the Americans and Vietnamese are presented in figure 8.3. The similarities in profile are readily apparent.

Again it may be necessary to make the point that a high degree of sharing does not mean that there are no significant differences

NEO big five factors and facets (typical item)	Americans Below av | Above av -2.0 -1.0 0 1.0 2.0	Vietnamese Below av | Above av -2.0 -1.0 0 1.0 2.0
Extroversion		
Cheerfulness (I look at the bright side)	|====	|=
Friendliness (I make friends easily)	|===	|==
Assertiveness (I take charge)	=|	==|
Activity level (I am always busy)	==|	===|
Gregariousness (I talk to a lot of different people)	===|	===|
Excitement seeking (I love excitement)	===:====|	====:====|
Agreeableness		
Altruism (I love to help others)	|====:=	|====:
Trust (I trust others)	|===	=|
Cooperation (I am easy to satisfy)	|====:	|====
Morality (I stick to the rules)	|====:=	|====:====
Sympathy (I suffer from others' sorrows)	|==	|==
Modesty (I consider myself an average person)	=|	|==
Conscientiousness		
Dutifulness (I try to follow the rules)	|====:====	|====:====
Self-efficacy (I excel at what I do)	|====:	|===
Achievement (I set high standards)	|====:=	|===
Self-discipline (I get to work at once)	|==	|=
Orderliness (I like to tidy up)	|====	|====
Cautiousness (I avoid mistakes)	|===	|====:
Neuroticism		
Immoderation (I go on binges)	:====|	==:====|
Self-consciousness (I only feel comfortable with friends)	=:====|	:====|
Anxiety (I fear for the worst)	=:====|	====|
Anger (I get angry easily)	===:====|	=:====|
Depression (I often feel blue)	:====:====|	===:====|
Vulnerability (I panic easily)	:====:====|	=:====|
Openness		
Artistic interests (I believe in the importance of art)	|====:=	|====
Intellect (I like to solve complex problems)	|==	=|
Emotionality (I experience my emotions intensely)	|==	|
Imagination (I enjoy flights of fantasy)	|=	===|
Adventurousness (I like to visit new places)	|=	=|
Liberalism (I believe criminals should receive help)	=:====|	==|

r between American and Vietnamese scores = 0.91

Figure 8.3   Vietnamese and American NEO facet means.

between the Vietnamese and the American. Because the sample sizes are of good size (512 Oregonians in Goldberg's sample), mean differences of approximately two-tenths of a standard deviation are significant. If we compare Vietnamese Americans with U.S. Americans across facets, we find that the Vietnamese are significantly different at the 0.05 level in 25 of the 30 comparisons.

Comparison of Vietnamese and American Mean Facet Scores

The Vietnamese are consistently lower than U.S. Americans on *openness*. Openness refers to the degree to which a person pursues complexity, change, and difference, as opposed to being motivated to avoid these and to pursue sameness, regularity, and the familiar (McCrae and Costa 1997a). In speculating about possible explanations for the Vietnamese Americans' low scores on all the *openness* facets, one thinks first of the predominantly traditionalistic nature of Vietnamese society—a society in which social structure, culture, and personality have been oriented toward conformity with a hierarchical social order that is assumed to be natural and unchanging. Many of the *openness* items are semantically similar to the value items that make up the personal exploration clusters of *individualism*.

Interestingly, Vietnamese Americans were almost half a standard deviation lower than the American norms on the NEO facets of *competence*, *achievement striving*, and *self-discipline*. This result is surprising in view of the literature describing numerous Asian groups, including the Vietnamese, as particularly conscientious in these very regards (e.g., Caplan et al.1989, Zhou and Bankston 1994), attributing Vietnamese and other recent Southeast Asian immigrants' educational and economic success in large part to Vietnamese cultural values of hard work and achievement in service of the family. However, as argued earlier, the achievement striving of the Vietnamese is more affected by the wish to secure status and security for the family than a personal need to excel at work. The results here are similar to the value results reported earlier, which found no strong differences between the Vietnamese and the Americans on the *industry* versus *relaxation* dimension. The Vietnamese also show a higher profile with respect to *neuroticism* than the Americans, especially with respect to *vulnerability* and *anxiety*. With respect to *impulsiveness*, however, the Vietnamese seem psychologically healthier than the Americans. Other studies of Vietnamese-American personality have also found elevated levels of depression and anxiety (Rumbaut 1989, Rumbaut 1985), predictable from the war traumas and migration-related stresses the Vietnamese Americans have endured.

The Relation of Values to Personality Characteristics

Table 8.4 presents the correlations for the Vietnamese between the six dimensions of the NEO and 58 value clusters. Some of the relations between the two have already been discussed. *Openness* has its strongest correlations with *individualism* and *industry* clusters. *Agreeableness* is most strongly related to the *altruism* clusters. *Conscientiousness* is most strongly related to *industry* clusters. *Neuroticism* has no strong correlations with any of the value clusters. These relations are fairly predictable from the semantic content of the items. But the structure of values that was found, while showing correspondences to the NEO dimensions, is really quite different from the NEO structure. *Extroversion* and *neuroticism*, as dimensions, have no clear place in any of the three value dimensions. *Conscientiousness* is positive correlated with the *industry* end of the pole, but not especially negatively correlated with the *relaxation* pole. Correlations with *agreeableness* are sprinkled over all the value dimensions. It seems fair to say that the two sets of data present partially similar pictures of the Vietnamese, with the pictures organized differently.

Which brings us back to a question raised earlier—to what degree is NEO personality data simply a reflection of the effect of values on self-report for group averages? Clearly, it is too strong to say that when dealing with group profiles, the NEO measures nothing but the semantic goodness of the items that make up the scales. For example, the higher neuroticism scores of the Vietnamese would seem to reflect something that is not related to differences in values. But it is not wrong to say that NEO group profiles are *strongly* value influenced. *Agreeableness* and *conscientiousness* are good, and they are most highly rated by both Americans and Vietnamese. *Neuroticism* is least highly rated by both Americans and Vietnamese. For *extroversion* and *openness* the result depends on the facet; *artistic interests* is highly rated, *liberalism* is not highly rated, *cheerfulness* is highly rated, *excitement seeking* is not highly rated, and so on.

The argument being made here is that both the value questionnaire and the NEO give information about group values when group means are used. The two questionnaires have some overlapping semantic content. There are consistent patterns of correlations between the two questionnaires; the Stewart-Love canonical redundancy index, which is a measure of the proportion of information that is accounted for in one matrix from the information in the other matrix, has a value of 0.45 predicting from the 58 value clusters to the 30 NEO facets. Both types of data show the effect of value universals, and both also show effects of unique cultural differences, as exemplified by the higher ratings of Americans on *openness*, which is part of the American *individualistic* value orientation.

This then raises a second question: If both questionnaires give a picture of group values, why do they have different structures—in the case of values, three dimensions of *individualism, altruism*, and *industry*, in the case of the NEO, five dimensions of *extroversion*,

Table 8.4   Correlations between NEO and values—Vietnamese data

Value Marco Clusters	NEO Personality Characteristics				
	Extroversion	Agreeableness	Conscientiousness	Neuroticism	Openness
Indivualism versus collectivism					
Individualism					
Personal exploration	*0.36*	−0.10	0.03	−0.04	*0.33*
Self-satisfactions	*0.34*	−0.07	0.00	0.02	*0.34*
Self-determination	0.27	0.17	0.21	−0.11	*0.35*
Collectivism					
Social morality	0.09	*0.30*	0.24	−0.07	0.06
Personal morality	0.20	*0.36*	*0.30*	−0.12	0.26
Circumspection	−0.03	*0.30*	0.25	−0.04	0.07
Altruism versus self-interest					
Altruism					
Eglitarianism	0.20	*0.46*	*0.35*	−0.15	*0.38*
Social amelioration	0.14	*0.37*	*0.30*	−0.13	0.26
Social adjustment	0.15	0.19	0.22	−0.09	0.24
Self-interest					
Success	*0.31*	−0.12	0.01	0.01	0.15
Self-advancement	*0.32*	0.05	0.19	−0.13	0.18
Belonging and being approved of	*0.30*	0.11	0.17	−0.05	0.22
Industry versus relaxaation					
Industry					
Striving	*0.35*	0.22	*0.31*	−0.19	*0.39*
Diligence	0.20	*0.38*	*0.42*	−0.16	*0.33*
Canniness	0.19	0.25	*0.31*	−0.05	0.22
Relaxation					
Amusements	0.23	−0.28	−0.17	0.05	0.10
Disengagement	0.00	−0.10	−0.13	0.15	−0.01

agreeableness, conscientiousness, neuroticism, and openness? A plausible answer is that the difference is the result of the fact that the *tasks* given to the respondent are different; in the case of the NEO, respondents rate *themselves*, while on the value questionnaire respondents rate something more abstract—whether something is *good*. When rating what is good in the world, the social dimensions of life— *individualism* and *altruism*—become relevant. In contrast, the NEO focuses on how one acts—the degree to which one is active, how well one treats others, how hard one works, and so on. The NEO organizes the respondents' ratings around one's sense of oneself as an agent, not around the problems of social life. So despite the similarity in content, asking people to rate themselves elicits a different structure than asking people to rate how good something is.

One final comment about the relations between the NEO and the value dimensions: Examination of the correlations between NEO and the value dimensions shows a clear pattern in which, when NEO components are correlated with clusters on one end of a value dimension, they are uncorrelated with the cluster at the other pole. For example, *extroversion* is correlated with the clusters that make up *individualism*, but uncorrelated with the *collectivism* clusters. This pattern holds throughout table 8.4. This indicates a phenomenon that Oyserman et al. (2002) noted—what appears to be a bipolar value dimension with respect to correlations of value items with each other can break into two dimensions with respect to correlations of value items with external measures like the NEO facets. Under such circumstances, it seems prudent to bifurcate the value dimensions when correlating them with other kind of data. Theoretically, these results indicate that the value components found earlier are not psychologically integral dimensions. One cannot be both short and tall, and if tallness is positively correlated with something, shortness will be negatively correlated with it. But one can be both happy and sad, and if happiness correlates positively with something, one cannot always predict that sadness will be negatively correlated with it. In chapter 4 the value dimensions were described as contraries, not contradictories. This appears to be both a psychological and a semantic fact.

Chapter 9

The Japanese

Our Japanese respondents were contacted through letters and acquaintances. All were born in Japan, speak Japanese as their first language, and are citizens of Japan. Of the 61 respondents, 43 percent also speak English. Sixty-five percent are female. The mean age of the sample is 36.8 and most of the sample report middle comes. The results of a second sample of 205 Japanese college students have also been made available through Yasusuke Minami at Seijo University. The results reported later are for the original sample unless otherwise stated. The Japanese questionnaire went through several translations into Kanji.

Like chapter 8, this chapter on the Japanese contains both quantitative and qualitative ethnographic material. The relation between the values findings and the ethnographic material is in greater tension than in the Vietnamese case. Despite the reputation of the Japanese people as collectivistic, the quantitative material does not indicate that the Japanese are significantly more collectivistic than the Americans. One major way of coming to terms with this finding is presented later, involving the complexities of what-counts-as-what. This in turn brings up issues concerning the locus of values—are they in the person or in roles and other institutions? These two issues remain central to the rest of this book.

Some material on Japanese values has been reported in table 6.1. In this table it can be seen that 2 of the top 10 Japanese items are directly concerned with the avoidance of war. The trauma of the Second World War has apparently left a strong imprint. As Benedict foresaw in the *Chrysanthemum and the Sword* in 1954, "Japan's real strength which she can use in remaking herself into a peaceful nation lies in her ability to say of a course of action, 'That failed,' and then throw her energy into other channels" (p. 304).

The majority of the other items in table 6.1 deal with interpersonal matters; *having close supportive friends, making friends, having someone I can really talk to*, and *having love*. The remaining items— *being healthy, treating human life as precious, having a positive outlook on life*, and *enjoying life*—focus on quality of life. The picture indicated by these top values is of an orientation toward social relatedness and life satisfactions—what Benedict described as the circle of *human feelings*.

Figure 9.1 presents the difference between the Japanese profile for the 58 value clusters and the Three Society average. Unlike the Americans, who have a strongly individualistic profile, and unlike the Vietnamese, who have a strongly collectivistic profile, the Japanese are not distinctive with respect to any of the three value dimensions. They are more distinctive with respect to some of the 58 value clusters, with higher than average ratings on *sleeping, eating,* and *drinking,* and on *avoiding war* and lower than average ratings on *being religious* and *being a leader.* The high value on sleeping, eating, and drinking has been commented on by a number of observers (Benedict 1945, Caudill and Plath 1966). The relatively low evaluation of religion has also been discussed in the literature (Nakane 1970), as has Japanese pacifism since the Second World War (Vogel 1979) and the avoidance of overt attempts to take the lead from others (Lebra 1976). The small differences find between Japanese and Americans on the *individualism* versus *collectivism* dimension are consonant with the Osyerman et al. meta-review, which found inconsistent results across studies. In another review study, Takano and Osaka (1999) found that among 11 questionnaire studies, in only 1 was there positive evidence for greater Japanese collectivism, while in 7 studies there was no difference and in 3 studies greater *individualism* among the Japanese was found. For behavior-experimental studies, two found no difference, while two found greater *individualism* among the Japanese; one Asch type conformity experiment in which the Japanese had a lower conformity rate than Americans, the other a prisoner's dilemma study in which the American subjects showed a higher level of cooperation than the Japanese. The complex situation of greater Japanese *collectivism* is taken up at length later in this chapter.

A more distinctive picture of Japanese values appears in the correlations between specific value items. In comparing correlations of other items with *promoting the values of my culture*, for example (table 9.1), the Japanese have one group of items that concerns liberal national policies and welfare, a second group that relates to family obligations, a third that concerns planning for the future, a fourth that involves harmony with nature, a fifth that involves relaxation and quiet, a sixth that is about group cooperation, a seventh that is about feeling sure of oneself, and an eight that is about having a world free of war. The overall picture is of a rich and diverse set of values—liberalism, family,

Difference Japan - average

Individualism versus collectivism

Individualism

Av. greater | Japan greater

−1.0 −0.5   0   0.5   1.0

Having time alone	|==
Understanding science	|=
Liking art and literature	|=
Being relaxed and enjoying life	|
Being creative	|
Being optimistic	=|
Being open to change	=|
Self-fulfillment	=|
Resisting authority	==|
Feeling sure about myself	==|
Choosing my own goals	==|
Having love and a satisfying sexual life	==|
Sexual freedom	===|
Living a life of adventure	===|
Having fun	==:====|

Collectivism

Being careful	|===
Being thrifty	|===
Defending my country	|===
The US military,the death sentence, National Security	|==
Being respectful and polite	|==
Maintaining tradition	|=
Having law and social order	|=
Working for the group and doing what others expect of me	|
Being sexually restrained	=|
Having a close-knit family	==|
Being religious	:====|

Altruism versus self-interest

Altruism

Avoiding war	|====:==
Living in harmony with nature	|====
Being able to adust	|===
Public schools, the UN, health care	|==
Respecting others' feelings	|==
Treating people equally	|==
Finding meaning in life	|==
Having close friends	|
Controlling myself	|
Being honest and genuine	=|
Working for social improvement	==|

Self-interest

Market competition, economic growth, capitalism	|====:
Keeping fit	|=
Having nice things, good looks, taste, success, etc.	|
Being liked and belonging	|
Having social status	==|
Being prosperous	==|
Being ambitious and competitive	:====|

Industry versus relaxation

Industry

Being orderly and regular	|==
Being persistent	|=
Being responsibility	|
Planning for the future	|
Being practical and realistic	=|
Pursuing knowledge and being well informed	=|
Working hard	===|
Having high standards	====|
Being a leader	=:====|

Relaxation

Sleeping, eating, drinking alcohol	|====
Believing in omens, mysticism, dreams, luck, psychics	|====
Enjoying comics, board games, sports	|=
Being detached and accepting one's fate	|=
Watching movies, tv, eating out	|

Figure 9.1   Comparison with Japanese to Three Society average for 58 value clusters.

Table 9.1   Top 20 correlations with *promoting the values of my culture*

r	Japanese	r	Americans
0.41	Liberal political policies	0.30	Observing religious holidays
0.34	Social planning	0.28	Taking part in ceremonies
0.28	National heath care	0.23	Being religious
		0.21	Having strong religious faith
0.27	Having deep respect for parents and grandparents	0.20	Doing what God wants me to
0.26	Not dishonoring my family	0.26	Preserving the family name
0.24	Fulfilling family obligations	0.20	Using firm discipline with children
0.31	Planning for the future	0.19	Having big family gatherings
0.25	Being prepared	0.17	Not getting divorced
0.24	Not giving up	0.17	Having and raising children
0.29	Having emotional ties with the natural environment	0.39	Having strong traditions
0.27	Living in harmony with nature	0.25	Maintaining old traditions
0.27	Being relaxed	0.21	Having authority over others
0.45	Having peace and quiet	0.20	Being obedient
0.25	Getting along with others through mutual concessions	0.20	Having a secure job
0.24	Going along with group decisions	0.19	Having a work routine
0.25	Feeling sure about myself	0.24	Standing during the national anthem
0.32	Saying what I think	0.18	Marrying someone from my own ethnic group
0.30	Having a world free of war		
0.26	Defending my country	0.18	Having a well-organized society
		0.18	Not getting involved with someone of bad reputation

future planning, nature, relaxation, group importance, self-assurance, and peace. Each seems to represent a theme of Japanese cultural discourse on the level of national commentary. Together they apparently create a sense of "We Japanese" that shows up in the correlations between "the values of my culture" and other values.

In contrast, the Americans have two large groups of items; one concerned with religion and faith, the other with preserving the family. There are also items involving tradition, hierarchy, and work. The overall impression is that these items reflect American political rhetoric about values; those who highly value promoting American values also value highly religion, family, work, and hierarchy. These more collectivistic values are part of conservative political discourse. It seems somewhat ironic that Americans promote a more collectivist conception of their cultural values than the Japanese do of theirs.

Another item that shows interesting correlational differences between the Japanese and Americans is *thinking well of myself* (table 9.2). For the Japanese, *thinking well of myself* is correlated with having jobs and financial security, being effective and intelligent, and having a good reputation. In contrast, the major groups of items for Americans predominately involve the self—self-esteem, self-understanding, the integrity of self, and so on. It is as if for the Americans, thinking well of oneself is primarily a reflexive matter—a matter of one's relationship

Table 9.2 Top 20 correlations with *thinking well of myself*

r	Japanese	r	Americans
0.40	Not being poor	0.40	Having a positive self image
0.24	Having a secure job	0.40	Feeling sure about myself
0.22	Being prosperous	0.23	Understanding myself
0.21	Having financial security	0.23	Improving myself
0.30	Catching on to things quickly	0.21	Having my own point of view
0.24	Being competent and effective	0.16	Being true to myself
0.23	Holding myself to high standards	0.22	Having a sense of humor
0.23	Being intelligent	0.22	Having fun
0.21	Developing new ideas		
0.38	Not getting involved with someone of bad reputation	0.22	Being able to express myself well
0.29	Having a good reputation	0.18	Having good looks
0.23	Being approved of	0.23	Being optimistic
0.30	Having comfort and contentment	0.16	Not giving up hope
0.21	Being alone	0.22	Developing ability and skill
0.20	Spending time by myself	0.20	Persevering to overcome difficulties
0.27	Seeking universal truths	0.16	Taking the initiative
0.27	Overcoming temptation	0.22	Having trust in others
0.26	Seeing the best in a situation	0.19	Being intuitive
0.23	Finding a mate with good moral and intellectual qualities	0.18	Maintaining a sustainable environment
0.21	Economic growth	0.17	Showing gratitude
		0.17	Having erotic pleasure

with oneself—while for the Japanese it is more a matter of having the right relationships with the world.

With regard to demographic variable, significant differences were not found by gender, religion (Buddhist versus none), or age. However, the first sample included very few college students, and comparing this sample with Minami's sample, which is composed entirely of college students, the older sample has at least a third of a standard deviation higher ratings on the clusters for *having love, understanding science, being careful, being honest and genuine,* and *living in harmony with nature.* The younger student sample has at least a third of a standard deviation higher ratings on *enjoying comics, having fun,* and *self-fulfillment.* The Japanese data is somewhat more homogeneous than the other two societies, and given the small effect of demographic variable throughout, these small differences are not surprising.

Japanese Collectivism

Looking at the results, it was surprising that the Japanese were not more like the Vietnamese. Both were expected to be collectivistic. The ethnographic literature is replete with material about how important groups are in Japanese society (Benedict 1945, Nakane 1970, Dore 1978, Lebra 1976). Japanese social groups—family, business, school—display observably strong solidarity and social control over the individual. Group norms tend to be highly codified and elaborate. A high degree of conformity to group norms is expected and typically deviants are strongly sanctioned. One is not supposed to be outspoken in one's group, and in fact most people avoid assertive leadership.

Lois Peak (2001), an educational psychologist and ethnographer, in describing the process of learning to become part of a group, says that for the Japanese school is *shudan seikatsu*, whereas at home their own desires and goals are not secondary to those of the group. Children are expected to participate enthusiastically in group activities and interact smoothly and harmoniously with others. To be selfish, or excessively assert independent desires and to want to have things one's own way, is termed *wagamama*. While considered part of human nature, it is not permitted to influence individual behavior in a group setting. Individuals are expected to assume appropriate attitudes and behavior, like a suit of clothes, for the duration of their active participation in the group (p. 144).

This picture of strong restraints on personal desires is also supported by questionnaire survey data. Kashima et al. (1995) developed sets of questionnaire items to measure collectivism, agency, and assertiveness. Items consisted of statements that respondents rated on Likert agreement scales. Example *Collectivism* statements are as follows:

> I am prepared to do things for my group at any time, even though I have to sacrifice my own interests.
> I respect decisions made by my group.
> I stick with my group even through difficulties.

Example *agency* statements are as follows:

> I stick to my opinions even when others in my group don't support me.
> I do things my way regardless of what my group members expect me to do.
> I base my actions more upon my own judgments than those of the group.

Assertiveness statements are as follows:

> I assert my opposition when I disagree strongly with the members of my group.
> I don't say anything even when I am dissatisfied with a decision made by my group (reversed).
> I often pretend to agree with the majority opinion in my group (reversed).

With respect to these three scales, the Japanese were half a standard deviation higher on the *collectivism* scale and almost a full standard deviation lower on the *agency* and *assertiveness* scales. The point should be stressed that these questionnaire items are predominately about what one *does*—how one normally acts or thinks one should act—not about personal values.

The Fujita and Sano Effect

At first look, the finding of no great difference between Americans and Japanese with respect to *individualism* versus *collectivism* on the value questionnaire and the finding of large differences with respect to *individualism* in ethnographic observations and in Kashima et al.'s survey research seem highly contradictory. Undoubtedly, part of the problem is the tendency in the social sciences to think of cultural differences as differences in values. However, treating cultural differences as value differences may not be restricted to social scientists. An ethnographic example may be helpful here. The following is a description of two Day Care centers; one in Japan—a suburb of Tokyo—and the other in a city in Wisconsin (Fujita and Sano 1988).

The children come from similar middle-class backgrounds. Both schools have about a 9 to 1 student teacher ratio. The teachers are almost all women. Children range in age from two to five and are organized in classes by age group. Most children spend the entire day at the school. The physical buildings and classrooms of the schools are similar. Daily schedules are also similar, including group activities (singing, painting, reading a story, dancing), snack, nap, lunch, and free play.

Classroom activities are structured differently in the two schools. The American school tends to break each class into smaller groups, and each of the teachers or teacher's aids coordinates the little group's activities. After about 15 minutes the children rotate and engage in a different activity. The children are constantly asked to choose from a list of two or three activities. The teachers believe that giving choices to children will help them to engage in the activity because they were not forced to do anything. In the Japanese school there is only a single activity in each classroom, and if there is more than one teacher they all help with that activity. However, in the Japanese school all the children are not expected to engage in the group activity, and it is quite permissible for children to play off by themselves or in small groups, or just to run around. This is not permitted in the American school.

The techniques of discipline are different as well. The American school uses "time-outs"—when a student is being distracting or difficult, the teacher pulls the child out of the group to sit quietly. After five minutes or so the student is allowed to rejoin the group. If the child has really misbehaved, the teacher will ask the child why he or she was disciplined, and if the child acknowledges fault, the child can return to the group and resume activities. The Japanese teachers do not directly discipline their children, but instead try to distract and divert the child with the goal of changing the child's mood rather than teaching right and wrong.

At both schools a hot lunch is served. In the American school the lunch is served in a common luncheon. Teachers eat with the children. Each food item is put on a large plate and passed around to the children who are asked to take some. If they do not like it, the teachers ask them to "at least try it." The American teachers encourage the children to talk and be sociable. No one ever feeds a child, no matter how young, because it is thought that this would lead to excessive demands for attention and giving up trying to feed themselves. After meals teachers will ask for volunteers to help clean up. Children like to be chosen and teachers rotate their selection of who gets to help.

In Japan the food is served in the classrooms. Among the oldest children, a boy and a girl are assigned by the teachers the task of setting the table and serving the plates and bowls that are already filled with food. This task rotates through the group, and children take pride in doing it as a sign of being a "big child."

Fujita and Sano say that one of the striking differences between the schools in the way children are moved from one activity to the next is that the American instructors rely primarily on verbal instructions, while the Japanese instructors rely more on the children's understandings of what to do. They have songs and musical chimes for the beginning and ending of various activities, such as snack time, washing hands, and brushing teeth. Generally the Japanese children seem to know what they are supposed to do next and help each other, while the American children are constantly bombarded with instructions. The American children also spend a lot of time getting into lines. The Americans believe that children should know not only what they are doing, but why they are doing it, otherwise they are just being taught blind obedience.

Major values in both schools are independence and becoming more adult and able to take care of oneself. Other values shared by both schools are that the children should feel secure and be comfortable and enjoy themselves. They should also learn cultural activities such as songs and games, as well as learn about language and writing and develop greater social skills. All of this is directly institutionalized in the various cultural practices described earlier.

There are also similarities in the cultural beliefs that are part of the cultural model of the situation. Obviously, children are understood to be in need of instruction, able to learn, different in their ages and skills, in need of protection, and so forth. There is a strong tendency for the American teachers to be more concerned about leaving children alone and unsupervised, especially in play outside the school. This may be a realistic assessment of the dangers to the child in the American environment. However, there are differences in beliefs about children between the two schools. The Japanese expect children to learn most easily by example, while the American teachers feel it is important for the child to learn from verbal instruction. The Japanese have greater trust that the child will grow out of its childish ways and that one can let the child grow at its own pace.

Fujita and Sano showed videotapes of the Japanese school to the American teachers and the American school to the Japanese teachers. Both the American and Japanese teachers were strongly impressed, and not favorably, with the differences between the schools. Summarizing Fujita and Sano:

(1) The Americans felt that the Japanese school is too noisy and even chaotic because of all the different things that are happening in the same classroom. This makes them worried that the environment is not safe for the children.

(2) The Americans felt that the Japanese teachers are not working with the children, but around them by preparing things for them, or just playing with them.

(3) The Americans thought that feeding of children, especially three-year-olds, is a mistake because it would spoil them.

(4) The Americans believe they are teaching children to think on their own and the Japanese are not. They give their children choices and explain things, but the Japanese do not. They believe they are being sensitive the children's individual needs by giving them choices. But because the children are little, teachers must always be in control of the process.

(5) The Japanese thought the Americans try to treat children as adults. Children are dressed as adults in clothes that make it difficult for them to go to the bathroom and that are not loose and soft, but tight and hard. Children at lunch are given adult plastic glasses, which are giant-sized for a child. This seems unreasonable to the Japanese; childhood is a separate stage and children have their own world and we should respect that and not impose on them.

(6) The Japanese criticized the Americans for not playing with children and not joining in their world and communicating with them in ways they understand. This seems lazy to the Japanese. In general, the Japanese see the Americans as strict and rigid.

(7) Fujita and Sano (1988) note that both the American and Japanese teachers underplay the similarities between the two day-care centers. Although the American teachers talk about the high ratio between teachers and children at the Japanese day-care center, this entirely ignores the numerical fact that the ratio for younger children is the same for both centers. Similarly, the Japanese do not comment on the affection that the American teachers physically demonstrated, such as hugs and kisses; the Japanese teachers describe the Americans as being strict and rigid (p. 91).

Thus, although the values are very similar and the general ideas about children are similar, the response of each group to the videos of the other group is shock at how different the other group is. But if the values are similar, where does the sense that the values of the two preschool are different come from?

There seem to be two major sources of the differences. The first is that values can be the same but what is evaluated can be quite different. Both sets of teachers want the child to become an adult. The Japanese evaluate letting the children have their childish ways as helping the child grow up. The Americans evaluate their constant verbal directions and explanations as helping the child grow up. The value is the same but differences in specific beliefs about the nature of children makes it seem to the Americans that the Japanese do not value independence while to the Japanese it seems that the Americans do not value childhood.

In this case there is some difference in belief. In other cases the differences only seem to involve how values are linked to practices. The Americans do not think that the Japanese give the children enough choices. The Japanese think the Americans do not really let the children make their own choices. The Japanese let children decide for themselves whether they want to join in an activity, and if a child wants to go off and do something else, that is permitted. To them this is clearly giving the child choice. The Americans experience this as chaotic. The Americans present the child with an array of choices of what game or activity they want to do, and then expect them to do it. To them this is clearly giving the child choice. To the Japanese it seems overstructured and rigid, taking away from the child's autonomy.

What is different about the two preschools are their *normative practices*. Norms specify what should be done, where and when, by whom and to whom. Normative practices are actions that follow the norms. The reason the relatively small differences in normative practices are responded to so sharply and with such criticism seems to be the following: *the viewer looks at what the person from the other society is doing, notices a regular difference, and then imagines that the person doing that thing has the values—or lack of values—that would have to be the case if the viewer were to do the same thing.* For an American teacher to feed a three-year-old would be to fail to try to help it reach an adult standard that the child can and should reach. This is obviously not a good thing to do. So if a Japanese teacher feeds a three-year-old, it seems it must be the case that the teacher does not value children becoming independent. But the inference is wrong.

In the same way, the Americans cannot see that the Japanese teacher expects children to make their own choices about whether to engage in the group activity or do its own thing, and that letting them make their own choices is part of respecting them as autonomous beings. The Americans simply do not frame what is happening that way. They frame what is happening as the teacher's losing control and not caring enough to keep order.

The point, once made, is obvious. Most values are relatively abstract schemas and very different actions can be framed as fulfilling or not fulfilling a value. Each society, in institutionalizing values into action systems, makes its own interpretive linkage about which values apply to which norms and practices. Outsiders, however, do not know which value is being linked to what norms and actions. Perhaps it is difficult for people to realize that the relation of values to actions is not that of a rigid designator such as a person's name, but rather a learned perspective about what-counts-as-what. Just because someone watches TV a lot does not mean that they really value watching TV—it may be that they just have nothing better to do.

In the case of the teachers viewing the videotape of day care in a different society, the teachers adopt their own cultural ways of construing and their own cultural perspective to interpret what is happening. Although the values and goals of the teachers in the two schools are quite similar, differences in how things are construed are great enough to give rise to the teachers perceiving large differences in values between the two social systems.

The differences between the American and Japanese day-care centers, I believe, are typical of the differences to be found when comparing cultural practices from different societies—families, business, religious groups, and so on. *The big differences are not in values, but in the interpretation of what-counts-as-what.* Difference in personal values between societies exist but tend to be small. About money, people are sophisticated; they know that in one society bills are large and red and have big numbers printed on them, while in another society bills are small and green and have small numbers printed on them, but that both kinds of bills function the same way. But this is not the case for what counts as independence on the part of children in day-care centers, or what counts as babying a child, or what counts as being natural. Both societies value independence. Teachers in both societies have the goal of helping children become independent, but observers from the other country cannot see this because they frame what-counts-as-what differently.

The Fujita and Sano story can be compared to the problems involved in trying to understand how is it that Japanese values are not highly collectivistic, yet within many institutions the cultural practices of the Japanese can reasonably be called collectivistic? Japanese cultural practices seem to the Japanese appropriate and correct—how one should behave in the world. Americans see these practices and think that the Japanese must have personal values that correspond to the values that would motivate them to act like the Japanese. But the world is not that simple. Japanese personal values on *collectivism* are not demonstrably higher than American personal values on *collectivism*.

The Relation between Values and Institutionalized Practices

This raises a further question: If the Japanese do not personally value collectivism very highly, what is the relation of Japanese personal values to collective cultural practices in Japan? Before trying to answer this question, certain other facts about Japanese culture need to be discussed. First, not all of Japanese life involves the cultural practices of *shudan seikatsu*. As Peak (2001) points out, the world of school contrasts greatly with the world of the family.

By definition, life within the family is not *shudan seikatsu*. Without exception Japanese teachers and students denied that it could be described as a small *shudan*. In contrast to the English concept of "group," the defining characteristic of a *shudan* is not the number of people involved but the expectations governing their interpersonal behavior. Within the family, one can drop the strain of *ki o tsukau* (holding oneself carefully) and freely express one's own feelings, however self-centered, and expect understanding and indulgence of one's personal desires. In fact, the right to expect such indulgence of *amae* (dependency) is the primary characteristic of an intimate or private environment, and without it a Japanese family would not be considered worthy of the name (p. 147).

The Japanese are quite aware of the contrast and the conflict between these two different kinds of institutionalized practices. Gordon Mathews has written (1996) about the different ideas the Japanese have about *ikiga*, translated in Japanese dictionaries as "something to live for, the joy and goal of living." The question "What's your *ikigai*?" is glossed as "What makes you feel life is worth living?" In researching the meaning of *ikigai*, Mathews found two strongly contradictory cluster of ideas, one focused on commitment to the group, the other on self-realization. Within the terms of this book, commitment to the group is a defining characteristic of *collectivism*, while self-actualization is a defining characteristic of *individualism*. Mathews sees these two opposing conceptions of iki-gai as "battling it out in Japanese media and minds over the direction of the future" (p. 21).

The trend since the end of the Second World War, Gordon feels, has been to shift the meaning of *ikigai* from *ittakan* to *jiko jitsugen*. Hidetada Shimizu (2001), however, argues that the dichotomy of characterizing the Japanese (or the Americans) is methodologically limited and conceptually inadequate to understanding everyday Japanese experience. In case studies of Japanese adolescents he finds that both individualistic and collectivistic concerns are salient and worrisome and that while in a state of tension, the two elements complement each other—one cannot individuate without being part of that which he or she individuates from, and one cannot participate without being individuated (p. 207).

Shimizu describes one of his informants, Yumi, a seventeen-year-old girl who thinks of herself as "two-faced" as in conflict about "real" (*honne*) versus "official" (*tatemae*) feelings. She knows she acts superficially to maintain her ties with peers, but does not want to be too honest because it leads to disagreement and isolation. She realizes many of her friends do the same thing, and that this is often the only way to maintain relationships. What compensates for this bind is having a best friend. Yumi says that because she has Kumiko as a friend, that is enough. Kumiko says that she will not share important things with her other friends, but just joke around with them. But to Yumi she will tell the truth, and only joke when she really enjoys joking. Yumi says she feels the same toward Kumiko, and that Kumiko is all the friend she needs (p. 213).

It is interesting that 2 of the top 10 Japanese values are *having close supportive friends* and *having someone I can really talk to*. As in the family, in friendship too there can be both a collective *we* and the permission to be oneself, uniting collective and individual themes.

The Japanese situation with respect to *collectivism* and the relation between values and practices contrasts with the Vietnamese case. Collective values are strongly endorsed among the Vietnamese and highly institutionalized in the family achievement syndrome. But it would be a great mistake to think that the Vietnamese family achievement syndrome exists just because the Vietnamese have strong values on achievement and family. A control case can be found in the world of Latinos in Los Angeles. Reese found that, like the Vietnamese in the United States, many Latino adolescents in their sample were children of immigrants, had strong family values, and also highly valued education and achievement (Reese, nd). However, they did not do well in school, did not spend much time doing schoolwork at home, and gave little attention to classroom learning. Reese found the relation between values and overt effort problematic. Almost all second-generation Latino high school students support the high value on education stated by either immigrant parents. The words are the same, but their actions belie their words (p. 4). Reese complains that this phenomenon is often reduced to differences in "values" with the standard Fujita and Sano explanation—if they are not working hard on education, they do not value education (p. 27).

There are many reasons for the low achievement of such groups; bad schools, disorganized and violent neighborhoods, lack of information about how to succeed academically, employment after school, and so on. One major component that is missing for most Latinos but present for most Vietnamese adolescents in the United States is a strongly institutionalized set of family practices that involve the child doing homework with parental scrutiny and assistance and parental sanctions for failure to achieve in school. While the personal values of the Vietnamese and Latinos concerning education are similar, the institutionalized values and the associated norms are quite different. The difference this makes for the child's success in school is very significant.

In the Japanese case a situation exists in which there are strong and pervasive cultural practices involving collective effort but without strong collective values. In the Vietnamese case there is a situation in which there are strong and pervasive cultural practices involving family-based achievement along with strong personal collective family values that reinforce these practices. In the Latino case there are strong family-based collective values but no institutionalized normative cultural practices that teach and demand achievement. Trying to construct a model to fit these findings leads to Cancian's conclusion that *values, by themselves, have little direct effect on behavior*. In situations of change, in which alternative cultural practices must be chosen, values can be directly causally important. But since one can have cultural practices without strong values, as in the Japanese case, or strong values without the cultural practices, as in the Latino case, it is obvious that the values are not a simple reflection of cultural practices or vice versa. Discrepancy between personal values and cultural practices may frequently be the case. Continuing debate about this issue is frequently discussed under the "attitudes and behavior" rubric. The usual generalization is that the more specific the attitude, the better the prediction. Values, then, since they are very abstract and very general standards, would not be expected to be good predictors of behavior.

What, then, is it like for the Japanese to live in a world in which many kinds of interactions are marked by a strong collective orientation when, in fact, the individual does not have strong personal collective values? Shimizu discusses an important value term, *omoiyari*, defined by Lebra (1976) as an ability and willingness to feel what others are feeling and help them satisfy their wishes. This value is pervasively institutionalized in the cultural practices of many Japanese roles. For example, according to the Japanese script, it is improper to ask guests whether they want to be served coffee or tea. Instead the host should have found this out or be able to make a good intuitive guess. To ask the guests what they want is a breech of decorum, since it indicates a failure of *omoiyari*. Shimizu says: "Despite the overall affirmation of the value of *omoiyari*, most respondents considered that neither they nor other adolescent peers, nor adults, fully internalized or fulfilled this cultural ideal....I found ambivalent attitudes toward *omoiyari*" (p. 233). Speaking of one informant, Shimizu (2000) says,

> Enmeshed in a world of personal relationships in which appearances are often in conflict with what's below the surface, she still believes it's important to "make the most out of her hobby and interests" and to "express her opinions clearly...." Thus, despite the overall emphasis placed on the importance of *omoiyari*, her personal experience appears to be also filled with doubts, conflicts, and ambiguity. (Shimizu 2000)

In the Japanese data *respecting other people's feelings* is, as a value, strongly affirmed. The specific values *feeling the pain of others, showing gratitude, not deceiving others, being loyal to friends*, and *keeping secrets* are all rated highly. However, values relating to *collectivism* such as *being obedient, respecting authority, doing what others expect me to*, and *going along with group decisions* are more than half a standard deviation below other Japanese value items. The discrepancy is not with valuing treating others well, but with being required to do so because of the group. Shimizu's adolescents experience this conflict acutely, along with the feelings of dishonesty that come with thinking of oneself as someone who is behaving with consideration for others not because one is internally motivated to be a good person, but because one must.

There are implications of the idea that there are often discrepancies between practices and values with respect to the Markus and Kitayama thesis that the Japanese, because they have a collective culture, have *interdependent* selves unlike the Western *independent* self (Kitayama et al. 1997, Kitayama et al. 2000, Heine et al. 2001). The experiments of Markus and Kitayama show that there are important differences in the emotional responses of Japanese and Americans. For example, they find that Japanese subjects are more likely than Americans to focus on failure situations as relevant to self-esteem, while Americans are more likely to focus on success situations as relevant to the self-esteem (Kitayama et al. 1997). In a similar vein Kitayama et al. (2000) found that Japanese rate themselves as having more negative socially engaged emotions (feeling indebted, ashamed, guilty) than positive socially engaged emotions (feeling superior, proud, on top of the world), while Americans rate themselves as having more positive socially disengaged emotions than negative socially engaged emotions. In another experiment, Heine et al. (2001) found that when Japanese are given negative feedback on how well they did a task they persist in trying to master the task longer than Americans.

It is important to note that these experiments do not show that Japanese personal values are different from American personal values. Showing that the Japanese respond differently to certain events does not, by that fact, indicate that different values are involved. The interviews of Gordon and Shimizu present quite a different picture—of people with values similar to those of ordinary Americans but who face problems particular to their social worlds, and whose emotions are quite understandable given the different social and cultural worlds they live in.

Japanese History and Collectivism

Some thoughts about how the Japanese discrepancy between values and cultural practices arose might be helpful. Many specialists have pointed to the history of Japanese feudalism as an important component in creating Japanese national character. Japanese feudalism continued through the Tokugawa period (1603–1868) until the Meiji reform. The Meiji reform centralized the government and emphasized the symbolic role of the emperor. Rather than ushering in a new world of individualism and free-market entrepreneurialism, the Meiji reformers created business, school, and governmental institutions that emphasized the importance of the group over the individual and the nation over all. The collectivism involved in these reforms was not based on a high evaluation of collectivism per se, but on the believed *effectiveness* of a collective effort in catching up with the West. In a sense, the Meiji reform was still feudalistic in spirit. Unlike China and Vietnam, where there was a long and strong Confucian tradition of well-coded collectivist values that were thought to be the right for their own sake, collectivism in Japan after the Meji reform was valued for instrumental reasons; primarily because it made one's group competitive against other groups, whether the group was a nation or school or business.

Douglas Haring, a psychological anthropologist who worked a number of years in Japan, made a remarkable ethnographic discovery in a field trip to a small island several hundred miles off the southern tip of Japan called Amami Oshima. The people of Amami Oshima, although Japanese in language and physical type, never fell under the domination of the feudal lords that controlled so much of Japan from the eighth century on. Without feudal domination, the people of Amami Oshima remained open and easygoing, sentimental and even passionate in their outward behavior. They are, apparently, without the ideals and burdens of Japanese *shudan seikatsu* (Haring 1949).

Our speculation is that during its long period of feudalism Japanese society became increasingly collectivistic at the level of normative cultural practices. Social organizations were hierarchically subjected to institutional sanctions that enforced group conformity, respect for authority, and nonassertive interaction. Collectivist cultural practices became institutionalized in a wide variety of roles. While value terms, such as *omoiyari*, were linked to proper group behavior, unlike Confucian-oriented societies, these values were not connected to ethical doctrines. Thus Japanese *institutionalized* values tend to be oriented more toward organizational efficacy than toward ethics. Since the Second World War, it appears there has been further erosion of collectivist values. Collectivist cultural practices, however, having been strongly institutionalized in schools and businesses, remain less changed, so that Americans, observing Japanese cultural practices, make the kind of value attribution mistake observed by Fujita and Sano.

These historical speculations are supported by Takano and Osaka (1999). In their review, discussed earlier, they argue that the contradiction between the empirical findings of a lack of collectivistic values and the alleged evidence for Japanese collectivism can be explained in terms of historical reactions. They say that the gunboat diplomacy that led to the Meiji reforms caused Japan to become "obviously collectivistic" in education, civil law, police power, and so on in order to establish the tight control over the nation that was needed to face

imperialist expansion. This collectivistic way of doing things continued through the Second World War and then, faced with a devastated
economy, spread to the economic practices of lifetime employment,
enterprise unions, and so on. However, Takano and Osaka argue,
while the Japanese people adjusted their behavior to these critical
situations, and "appeared to possess a *tendency* to behave collectivis-
tically," they nevertheless "did not have a collectivistic *disposition*"
(Takano and Osaka 1999, pp. 327–328, italics added).

For me, the Japanese results were a worldview-altering experience.
The ethnographic data were so strongly indicative of Japanese collectivism that I could not believe the questionnaire results. This disso-
nance has been resolved by developing a model in which the relation
between personal values and cultural norms and practices is contin-
gent; in some cases the personal values of the participants fit the cultural norms and practices, in other cases they do not, or not well
enough. This perspective opens up perspectives to be explored in chapter 10 about the relation of values to cultural norms and practices.

Chapter 10

Institutionalized Values

Our Japanese results raised questions about the relation between personal values and institutions and group norms. This relationship is made even more complex by the existence of *institutionalized values*, sometimes called *normative* or *social values*. Institutionalized values are defined here as values that people agree *should* be valued in enacting some *role* or performing in some *group*. Consider, for example, the world of the military. Military roles are marked by distinctive social practices including the wearing of uniforms, the assignment of formal rank, the saluting of higher ranks by lower ranks, the obedience given to higher ranks, along with powerful sanctions for failure to follow these norms. These norms of behavior are tightly connected to institutionalized values of obedience, respect for rank, unit loyalty, courage, patriotism, and responsibility. These are the values people in the military should live by, whatever their personal values. In general, as part of one's cultural heritage, people learn which values apply to which roles. Typically, the relationship is direct and transparent—many institutionalized values are the same criteria by which performance in a role is judged. A value standard that is consensually used to evaluate role performance is said to be *institutionalized* (D'Andrade 2006).

The idea that there can be values that are not personal may seem counterintuitive. In the usual sense, values are something a *person* values. But we also know that bravery is an important value for the soldier role, that knowledge is an important value for the student role, and that competitiveness is an important value for entrepreneurial roles. These are important values that people in these roles should be guided by whatever their own personal values. Of course, it is best if people in the military do have respect for rank and bravery as personal values, and best if people in academia value knowledge, creativity, and finding out about the world. However, it is commonly recognized that often people have values that are incongruent with the institutionalized values of their roles.

One of the differences between psychologists and social theorists is the way they think about values. When psychologists speak of "group level" values (Smith 2004), they mean something different from institutionalized values. For psychologists, values are considered to be at the group level when individual values have been averaged to obtain a group profile. In contrast, institutionalized values are values that some collectivity holds. Just as any set of norms requires a collectivity to hold to these norms, so do institutionalized values require a collectivity that hold these values. It may be those who belong to some role or group, but they are not just stereotypes or group averages.

Most psychologists interested in values—Allport, Rokeach, Triandis, Schwartz—tend to think of values as characteristics of persons. In contrast, social theorists are more likely to think of values as characteristics of institutions. This project began in the psychological tradition, concerned with measuring the personal standards that individuals use to evaluate their worlds. But, as the research continued, more and more anomalies built up. If values were not very different around the world, why did ethnographic work describe such different value worlds? At first I thought this might be explained by the fact that the very top values in each society tend to be unique, as discussed earlier. But, while true, this effect is insufficient to account for the large ethnographic differences recorded for different societies. Then, based on the Japanese results and the Fujita and Sano study presented in chapter 8, it became apparent that different practices could be attached to the same values because what-counts-as-what can vary so greatly by culture. However, this second explanation was also insufficient to account for all the ethnographic data. For example, by all accounts, a paramount value of traditional India was purity. Purity does not seem to be a paramount value in modern America. This does not appear to be just a matter of what-counts-as-what, but rather a real value difference.

Some way into the data-collecting phase of this research the importance of distinguishing personal values from institutionalized values became clear, and then many of the anomalies could be sorted out by recognizing this difference. A search of the literature to discover the way in which this distinction has been handled produced few results. In the search—undoubtedly incomplete, given the large literature on values—a few empirical studies or theoretical discussions were found that focused on this distinction. When the distinction between institutionalized and personal values is mentioned, it is often dismissed as nothing more than the difference between the group average and the individual average. Many of these researchers say that "while various methods can be used to assess unit-level values, *organizations do not really possess values apart from the values of their members*" (italics added) (Meglino and Ravlin 1998, p. 357). Rohan (2000), in an extensive review of value study in psychology, notes that little attention has been given to the institutionalized versus personal value distinction, and discusses the lack of consensus about how to measure institutionalized values (p. 265).

Our position, contrary to those cited earlier, is that institutions, roles, and organizations do possess values apart from the personal values of their members. Institutionalized values are not just other people's perception of the values of other people, but are *collectively agreed upon value criteria that apply to role performance*. Rohan in her research on teachers used a measure of institutionalized values very close to the definition proposed here, which she describes as "teachers' perceptions of *their school's ideological value system...*" (italics added, p. 266). Using a modified version of the Schwartz value survey, she was able to show the fit between teacher's personal values and their institutionalized values strongly predicted subjective stress, job commitment, and job satisfaction. She notes, "Neither an index of fit constructed on the basis of personal value priorities and the school's principal's value priorities nor an index constructed on the basis of fit between personal value priorities and the average of all teachers' institutionalized value priorities could match this prediction" (p. 266).

An outstanding exception to the general dismissal of institutionalized values in the psychological literature can be found in a study by Rokeach of scientists (Rokeach 1979). Rokeach asked whether it was possible to identify the values of highly abstract, supraindividual social systems that sociologists identify as social institutions. To answer this questions Rokeach used five different measures. The first measure consisted of administering the Rokeach value survey to 152 faculty members at Michigan State and Wayne State universities from the physical, biological, and social sciences. Finding the three groups to have similar patterns of values, the mean ranking of the 36 Rokeach value items became the basic measure of the personal values of scientists. Rokeach also included the results from his value survey for a sample of 66 graduate students from the same universities, regarding these graduate students as inductees into the institution of science. From other Rokeach publications the value profile of the National Opinion Research Center (NORC) representative sample of 565 Americans surveyed in 1965 was included. The analysis presented later modifies the analysis presented in Rokeach's paper in collapsing the distinction between terminal and instrumental values and in adding the NORC sample.

Three measures of the institutionalized values for the role of scientist were constructed. The first was to give the same sample of 156 scientists the Rokeach value survey and ask them to rank *the values of science as an enterprise*. This might be called the insiders' conception of the institutionalized values of science. The second was to ask a sample of nonscientists, or outsiders, to rank the values of science as an enterprise—the outsiders' conception of the institutionalized values of science. The third measure was based on a content analysis of 80 editorials randomly selected from the 520 editorials published in *Science* from 1964 to 1973. Two coders were trained to judge the presence or absence of the 36 Rokeach items in the editorials. The total frequency for any one value was the total number of separate mentions of that value in the 80 editorials. The correlations of all 5 measures across the 38 value items are presented in table 10.1.

The results are a clear confirmation of the idea that the institutionalized values, attached to the role of the scientist, are different from but related to the personal values of scientists. The five measures form a single component dimension accounting for 67 percent of the variance. The "best" or "purest" measure of the institutionalized values of science is the content analysis of the *Science* editorials. The next two measures, the perceived values of science by nonscientists and the perceived values of science by scientists, also make good measures of the institutionalized values of science. The personal values of scientists are strongly related to these three measures of the

Table 10.1   Intercorrelations between five methods of measuring the values of science plus the NORC sample

	1.	2.	3.	4.	5.	6.
1. Content analysis	1.00	0.65	0.61	0.44	0.37	0.14
2. Perceived values of science by non-scientists	0.65	1.00	0.85	0.60	0.26	0.24
3. Perceived values of science by scientists	0.61	0.85	1.00	0.78	0.44	0.18
4. Values of scientists	0.44	0.60	0.78	1.00	0.74	0.31
5. Values of graduate students in science	0.37	0.26	0.44	0.74	1.00	0.26
6. Average of NORC sample	0.14	0.24	0.18	0.31	0.26	1.00

institutionalized values. The graduate students, while similar to the professors in their personal values, are less strongly related to the institutionalized values of science. In other words, scientists have strongly internalized the institutionalized values of science, graduate students somewhat less so, although they have internalized more of the values of science than ordinary folk as represented by the NORC sample. The specific values that differentiated science from the personal values of ordinary people were greater evaluation of being logical, imaginative, accomplishing things, having an exciting life, and being intellectual.

Barry Schwartz, a psychologist and social theorist, takes values to be principles, or criteria, for selecting what is good, better, or best. He maintains that social institutions embody individual values when the institution offers people roles that encourage behavior that display the values, and fosters conditions for the further expression of these value. A social order embodies a value to the extent that it promotes social institutions that embody the value. An individual's values are constrained by the social institutions and the social order in which that individual lives. Indeed, social stability is affected by the fitting together of personal values and institutional opportunities for their expression (1993, p. 153).

Here Barry Schwartz includes not only the idea that institutions embody values, but also the idea that an entire social order can embody values, as well as the hypothesis that social stability is affected by the congruence between personal values and social values. Shinobu Kitayama has a relevant theoretical position with respect to the relation of personal values to culture. He calls his position "the systemic view." According to Kitayama, every culture consists of a set of practices and meanings, laid out by generations of people who have created, carried, maintained, and altered them. People come to think, feel, and act with reference to local practices, relationships, institutions, and artifacts; to do so they must use local cultural models, which can become internalized. Each person tries to behave adaptively in the appropriate cultural context, and in the process different persons develop their own unique set of response tendencies, cognitive orientations, emotional preparedness, and structures of goals and values (Kitayama and Markus 1999, pp. 250–251).

According to Kitayama, personal values are *not* cultural values writ small. Nor are cultural values personal convictions writ large. Precisely because individualistic cultural values such as liberty, happiness, and autonomy are significant in an individualist culture such as the United States and are endorsed by all members of the culture they are not personal values. Instead, these values are significant because they have historically shaped the contemporary cultural system—the system of social institutions, conversational scripts and routines, daily practices, and lay theories (Kitayama 2002, p. 90).

Kitayama's term *cultural values* clearly refers to what are called here *institutionalized values*. I differ with Kitayama, who does not wish to call shared personal values *culture*. My position is that a society's cultural heritage *includes* both shared personal values as well as institutionalized values and so there is no reason not to call them both *culture*.

The Institutionalized Value Questionnaire

With respect to this project, two major questions concerning institutionalized values need to be answered. The first question is whether or not institutionalized values show the same dimensional structure as personal values. The second question concerns the relation between institutionalized values and personal values. To help answer these questions, a *roles and values* questionnaire was developed with the following format:

CIRCLE THE NUMBER WHICH CORRESPONDS TO HOW IMPORTANT EACH ITEM IS TO *BEING A DOCTOR*

Forty-three value items were selected from the 328 original items representing the main value clusters described earlier. Twelve well-known roles were chosen: *business person, doctor, employee, teacher, student, governor, father, mother, son, daughter, friend,* and *lover*. Six different questionnaires were constructed, each with 6 roles and 43 values items. The questionnaires were organized so that each role occurred in two questionnaires. Each questionnaire was administered to 10 UCSD undergraduates, resulting in every role being evaluated by 20 respondents. Although relatively small, this sample size was felt likely to be sufficient because the ratings were about the kind of cultural understandings that typically show strong consensus effects. This was supported by high group reliabilities: The group average of the alphas for the 12 roles was 0.97 (see chapter 5 for a discussion of group alphas).

The data was analyzed by first forming a table of the means for each of the 43 value items for each of the 12 roles. Seventeen items discriminated well between the roles, with standard deviations across roles greater than 0.44. These items were selected for use in a *correspondence analysis*. Correspondence analysis, like component analysis and principal components analysis, belongs to the single value decomposition family of statistical techniques (Weller and Romney 1990). Unlike component analysis or principal components analysis, correspondence analysis places both row and column variables in the same space. Originally derived for the analysis of contingency tables of frequency data, it has proven to be an effective and robust technique for a wide variety of applications (see earlier) (Romney et al. 1999, Greenacre 1993).

The results are presented in figure 10.1. The results strongly confirm the hypothesis that roles are associated with specific values, and also confirm the generality of the *individualism/collectivism* and *altruism/self-interest* dimensions, which are clearly apparent and which emerged without rotation. With respect to the relation of the personal values to institutionalized values, from figure 10.1 it can be seen that the position of the *self*—an individual's personal values— falls close to the center of the graph. More *collectivistic* and more *benevolent* are the family roles of *mother, father, son,* and *daughter.* More *individualistic* and *benevolent* are the roles of *lover* and *friend,* while the roles *teacher, doctor, employee,* and *business person* are higher on *self-interest.* The role of *governor* and the *typical American* are also higher on *self-interest,* and also more *collectivistic.* Overall, the *self* is slightly closer to the family roles than to any other cluster. The value profile for the personal values of the average individual does not fit exactly any of these roles, and is centered with respect to the *individualism/collectivism* and *altruism/self-interest* dimensions.

The distinction between institutionalized and personal values helps explain one of the perplexing conundrums mentioned earlier. To illustrate, let us take up again the case of Indian values, central in the work of Dumont and many other Indian scholars (Dumont 1980, Marriot 1990). Although there is disputation about whether purity is the prime value of traditional Indian society, or just one among several paramount values, the salience and importance of purity as a value in Indian culture is uncontested. What, one can ask, would happen if one surveyed individuals in India about their personal values? Such research has already been done. Based on use of the Schwartz value survey, we find a sample of Hindu teachers from Allahabad and Patna correlated with the worldwide average sample 0.88, while a Hindu student sample correlated 0.75 (Schwartz and Bardi 2001). These results would not lead us to expect the great difference in values from those of the West described again and again in ethnographies of India.

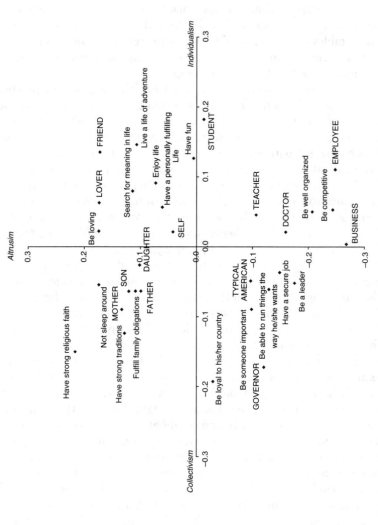

Figure 10.1 Correspondence analysis of roles and selected value items: American data.

Some of the ethnographic differences can be accounted for by noting that in India, what counts as pure versus impure is different from that in the West. Different groups of people, different foods, and different objects are understood in India to have different degrees of purity, and contact with materials of lesser purity is polluting and must be avoided, or, if unavoidable, cleansed by proper washing rituals. Purity in India is not just a very strong personal value; it is a value that, through the X counts as Y rule, applies to a truly vast range of things.

However, it is not just the strong personal value of purity and its wide range of instantiation that makes India different. Purity in India is a highly general and salient *institutionalized* value. Castes are ranked by purity. Each caste *should* avoid foods and people less pure. Purity is so extensively institutionalized in India that some social theorists consider it to be the primary ideological basis of Hindu society (Dumont 1980, p. 44). To cite Barry Schwartz again, "An entire social order embodies a value to the extent that it provides conditions that nurture social institutions that embody the value." Certainly in both traditional and modern India major social institutions embody the value of purity.

Purity in India is not only a pervasive social standard. Many observers have noted that it is also a deeply internalized personal value (Carstairs 1957). Indeed, based on conversations with people who have worked recently in India, it seems to be the case that while there is some diminution in the range of things that nowadays count as polluting, there is no diminution in the importance of purity as a personal value. More work on the degree to which current changes are seen in personal values, or in institutionalized social values, or in what-counts-as-what in India may help in furthering understanding of how social change works.

Returning to the problem of collective values among the Japanese, it seems highly likely that the collective practices of business and school described in the ethnographic literature are accompanied by strong social values attached to specific roles like that of student and employee. In her book *Beamtimes and LifeTimes* (1988), Sharon Traweek contrasts Japanese and American high-energy physics working groups. The American model for such research groups is that of a sports team. The leader, a senior physicist, is the coach who assigns tasks and decides on strategy for the postdocs and graduate students. While the atmosphere is informal, the actual organization is quite hierarchical, with the work crew left out of decision making and often not well informed about the conduct of the whole enterprise. There is a high value on winning—what counts as winning is making the big discoveries first. Ideas are considered private property, to be used by their owners for their best advantage. There is a very strict division of labor within the work group, and the members of the group face a constant conflict between giving all their time and effort to the group, which is what the team leader wants, and doing various kinds of work on their own and developing their own ideas, thereby gaining a reputation that will help get a job once the research project is completed.

The Japanese model is more like that of the Japanese *ie*, or household, where it is the obligation of each member of the household to maintain and increase the resources and prestige of the household and pass them on to the next generation. Status in the work group is determined by seniority, not competition. The division of labor is not strict, and all members contribute their point of view in discussion about what will be done. However, after listening to all members of the group and gauging their feelings, the senior person states a decision about the direction research should take, which is binding to all. If asked where the ideas for the project came from, the Japanese senior leader credits the members of the group, unlike the U.S. teams where the leader presents himself as producing the ideas, although admitting sometimes privately that the members of the team provided crucial ideas. The way in which the American postdocs are left to fend for themselves after the project is completed probably seems cruel to the Japanese. In their world, once admitted to the group, one will be taken care of to the extent possible. The quid pro quo for this is that the individual will give loyalty and commitment to the group.

At every point the two worlds are value saturated, but more by institutional than personal values. One might guess that a fairly large number of Americans would prefer the Japanese household model over the U.S. team model because it is more congruent with their own personal values. However, outside forces concerning funding support the team model, which probably fits the ideology of those distributing the resources better than the Japanese household model. The same is true in Japan, where research funds tend to be allocated by university and department rather than competitive grant applications. All of this makes a nice example of how ideologies can support upper-level decision-making processes that create institutional forms which embody particular institutionalized values. However, Traweek points out that these national differences, while pervasive, are not monolithic, and that there is variation both in Japan and the United States with respect to the organization of physics research work groups.

Turning back to Barry Schwartz's point that an entire social order embodies a value to the extent that it provides conditions that nurture social institutions that embody the value cited earlier, the question arises about the values that are embodied or institutionalized by a modern society such as the United States. Talcott Parsons argued that values have the capacity of generalizing individual reward and motivation systems across different roles and institutions. That is, the intrinsic motivational rewards an individual obtains from being an architect are probably quite different from the intrinsic motivational rewards of being a policeman or a mother. Modern societies have kinds of rewards that are general across different roles and institutions—for example, money and prestige. However, money and prestige are usually themselves granted because of value standards. Parsons argued that to function, societies needed a considerable degree of integration, and that one important kind of integration was brought about by the existence of an institutionalized value system that is general across roles. Without getting into debates about functionalism, a relatively simple empirical question can be asked about the degree to which a society has, or does not have, a generalized system of values.

Parsons thought that the most general institutionalized value characteristic of modern industrial and postindustrial societies was *instrumental activism* (Parsons and White 1964). That is, almost all the roles of a modern society such as the United States have institutionalized in them a strong value concerning *getting things done*. There are only a few roles available to Americans that might be said to have *withdrawing from the world into contemplation* (monks, intellectuals) as an institutionalized value.

Parsons's argument that *getting things done* forms a highly generalized value standard across many roles in modern societies seems right. However, instrumental activism appears to be one value in a system of values that lock together and reinforce each other. Just doing things is not enough. If one asks "what do I want my doctor to be—my architect, my plumber, my broker, my son, my professor, my student"—the answer is that they should be *competent* and *responsible*. Even further, as part of these roles, they should do some *good* in the world—not just be self-serving. Business people should treat their employees well, doctors should take care of their patients, teachers should be concerned about the welfare of their students, and so on. Even mothers and fathers should be competent—what could be worse than being found to be an incompetent mother? There is empirical evidence in the value data for the generality of these institutionalized values. Reexamining the role data, a number of value items were found that had high values across all roles. These items did not appear in figure 10.1 because, having high averages across all roles, they were not used in differentiating between roles. Table 10.2 below shows the mean ratings (unipsatized) for the roles of *business person, governor, employee, doctor, teacher,* and *student.*

Strange as it may seem, family and other intimate roles also have high ratings on these same value items (see table 10.3).

The overall picture is that all the roles examined here show the same pattern; whatever the role, it is important in the performance of that role to be a good person (responsible, honest, treats others well) who is self-directing (self-controlled, independent, and self-reliant), hardworking (persevering, hardworking), and competent (knowledgeable). All in all, this sounds like Weber's Protestant ethic. Based on the data here, it would seem that even the roles of *lover, friend, father, son, mother,* and *daughter* fall under the shadow of this ethic.

Table 10.2   Top 8 value items (ratings 0 to 4) for 6 occupational roles

Value Items	Business Person	Governor	Employee	Doctor	Teacher	Student
Be responsible	3.5	3.5	3.3	3.6	3.7	3.4
Be honest	2.8	3.5	3.4	3.5	3.5	3.0
Persevere to overcome difficulties	3.4	3.5	3.0	3.7	3.6	3.2
Treat others well	3.0	3.6	3.2	3.5	3.5	3.5
Have self-control	3.3	3.8	3.2	3.5	3.5	3.2
Be independent and self-reliant	3.4	3.4	3.0	3.6	3.4	3.3
Work hard	3.5	3.7	3.4	3.6	3.4	3.6
Be knowledgeable	3.3	3.4	2.9	3.9	3.7	3.2

Table 10.3   Top 8 value items (ratings 0 to 4) for self and intimate roles

Value Items	Friend	Lover	Daughter	Son	Mother	Father	Self
Be responsible	3.3	3.7	3.6	3.6	3.8	3.9	3.5
Be honest	3.6	3.9	3.5	3.5	3.7	3.7	3.7
Persevere to overcome difficulties	3.3	3.6	3.4	3.5	3.6	3.8	3.3
Treat others well	3.5	3.7	3.6	3.5	3.5	3.8	3.4
Have self-control	3.2	3.7	3.3	3.3	3.5	3.7	3.3
Be independent and self-reliant	3.1	3.5	3.5	3.3	3.4	3.6	3.6
Work hard	2.8	3.4	3.4	3.2	3.2	3.2	3.4
Be knowledgeable	2.6	3.2	3.4	3.0	3.2	3.3	3.5

On an anecdotal level, common cultural knowledge indicates that the standards of responsibility, self-reliance, hard work, and competence apply not only generally across roles, but apply with greatest force at the upper levels of different role stratification systems. That is, it is a general observation that within the hierarchies of business, politics, education, law, medicine, and the like, these criteria apply most strongly to those at the top. Those at the upper levels of various stratified role systems are theoretically more accountable to these general values than those at the bottom; however, often that results in disappointment brought about by irresponsible CEOs, untruthful presidents, incompetent full professors, politically motivated Supreme Court justices, and the like.

The Formation of Personal Values

In the beginning of this book a semantic and conceptual framework was set out for the study of values. This framework emphasized the importance of recognizing the several different senses of the term, and the reasonableness of privileging the definition of values as the sense of goodness over the definition of value as preference or the restricted sense of values as moral criteria. At this point it is possible to return to the problem of developing a conceptual framework for values with a more empirical feel for the nature of the beast.

When rating scales were sampled to determine the best scale to use, it was found that almost all the scales belonged to a single large component (table 3.2). "I value ___" and then later "___ is important to me" were selected because these scales had the highest component loadings, indicating that they are central foci in a semantic network involving the general evaluation of things in terms of their goodness.

Further information can be derived from the relations among these scales. For another look at this data, a correspondence analysis was performed on the rectangular matrix of scales and concepts. Correspondence analysis has the advantage of removing the first general component from a matrix, making it possible to explore other dimensions that were swamped by the first dimension in a standard principal components analysis. The full matrix for analysis consisted of 18 evaluation scales and 6 concepts. The results are presented in figure 10.2.

The concepts rated are in capitals. Both the placement of the rating scales and the concepts rated display dimensions which, like the other value dimensions, are contrasts rather than opposites. On the first

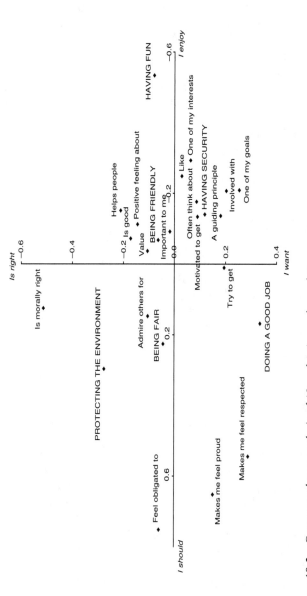

Figure 10.2 Correspondence analysis of 18 evaluative scales and 6 concepts.

dimension, scales that involve the sense that *I should* contrast with scales that have the sense *I enjoy*. On the second dimension scales that have the sense that something *is right* contrast with scales that involve the sense of something *I want*. It is notable that the scales in the center of the graph—*value having* and *important to me*—are the highest loading scales in the principal components analysis. This seems to be because these two scales are in the center of the contrasts between *I should/I enjoy* and *is right/I want*. Thus, for something to be rated high on the scale *I value having ___* or *___ is important to me*, it must not be something that is exclusively an enjoyment, or just a personal want, or just something that is thought to be right, or just something I should do. The meaning of the term *value* in normal speech partakes of all of these. In the same way the concept *being friendly* (also in the center of the graph) is rated highly on the value and importance scales because it is simultaneously something one should do, something that is enjoyable, something wanted, and something that is right. This means that when people say they value something highly, or that something is very important to them, they are rating this something highly not just on the basis of criteria concerning enjoyment or obligation or moral rectitude or desire, but as an integrated sum of all these.

People behave differently toward things depending on which of these facets is salient and whether or not all facets are present. Barth presents a nice ethnographic example of this in contrasting the way in which the Baktaman, a people of western New Guinea, and the Balinese, act with respect to generosity. The Baktaman are shy, unaggressive, and sensitive to the needs of others, minimizing conflict by accommodation. However, they do not conceptualize these ways of acting as valuable. Barth says he was unable to find a conception of generosity, consideration, or sociability in their moral discourse or their admonitions to their children. What they discuss is their fear of sorcery and the need to avoid inducing anger in others. The rational they give for their acts of sharing and amity is that it avoids angering others and, therefore, avoids being witched. Thus their preference and desire for peaceful interaction is not done because they feel it is intrinsically right, or because one is obligated to do it, or because it is especially enjoyable. As a result, there appears to be no culturally developed standards that say that generosity, consideration, and sociability are good. Barth says, "I think it would be false to impute to them (on the basis of their praxis) a concept of consideration, altruism, or tact [that represents] a generalized value with some such content as the mechanism or cultural force that generates this pattern of behavior" (1993, p. 38).

Barth contrasts this with the North Balinese, who on the surface are also generous, attentive, considerate, and sociable, and like the Baktaman, also behave in an amiable friendly way to avoid witch-craft. However, the Balinese live in a very different institutional world than the Baktaman. Among the Baktaman land is freely available to all; permission to hunt and collect in clan-owned territories is extended to anyone who requests it; most dwellings are communal; tools, equip-ment, and even items of personal adornment are made available on request. In contrast, among the Balinese most land is privately owned, production and exchange are aimed at securing a material advantage, and people wish to accumulate material goods. But it is the Balinese who "conceptualize, embrace, and give eloquent expression to the value of generosity and condemn greed, and who emphasize the per-centile of material goods that pass as gifts as a major component of their morality, admonishing that one should learn to give without regrets" (p. 41).

Barth rejects as an explanation that it is the very presence of the Balinese institutions of property and markets and competitive exchange that create the personal and institutional value of generosity—or at least, as he says, until someone provides "a coherent account of the actions and codifications by which such a dialectic is generated" (p. 41). Such an account is attempted here, although a great deal remains to be filled in. Our general hypothesis is that *values are always a compro-mise in a tension between opposing tendencies.* In the correspondence analysis of the rating scales two pairs of contrasting tendencies were found; *to do as one is obligated* to versus *to do what one enjoys doing,* and *to do what is right* versus *doing what one wants.* These are very general conflicts. And, in the dimensional analysis of a wide sample of value items a similar set of contrasting pairs was found; *collectivism* versus *individualism* and *altruism* versus *self-interest.* Without doing interpretative violence to the data *collectivism* can be aligned with *social obligation* and *individualism* with *doing what one enjoys.* The correspondence between *altruism* and *doing what is right* is very close, as is the correspondence between *self-interest* and *doing what one wants.* These are not the only ways one can interpret the relations between these pairs of dimensions, but certainly the degree of fit is notable.

Why should the data look like this? One answer is that value standards in many domains are a negotiated adjustment to a conflict. Consider as a simple example, the *industry* versus *relaxation* dimen-sion. Suppose one wishes to try to set the social standards for a work office. Not even Scrooge could mandate *nothing* but work for the whole work-day. There must be some time for people to relax, have a cup of coffee or at least a glass of water, stretch, and converse about various matters. What any office manager has to do is to set a standard somewhere between total work and total relaxation. And no matter where the institutionalized value standard is set, there will be constant conflicts—people spending too much time around the water cooler, or people pinned to a desk for too long. The value standard will be pushed back and forth by the friction of human interaction.

The conflict between the wish of management to get as much work done as possible and the wish of the workers to relax and enjoy themselves is an external conflict. It will give rise to institutionalized value standards, with all the attendant conceptualizations, labels, and negotiations about what-counts-as-what. If the conflict is entirely external, there will be no internalization of these standards. Now consider the case of someone who is self-employed. The conflict about how much to relax and how much to work is now an internal one. The standards the person develops will be internal and represent a personal value—a point along the *industry/relaxation* continuum that the person feels is right. The process of internalization has begun.

Most people are caught up in some degree of conflict about how much they should commit to the vast sea of social obligations they live in and how much they should commit to the pursuit of their own goals. Different people set the standard in different places. Different roles require different set points. Different situations require changing set points. The conflict is ubiquitous, which, I argue, is why the *individualism/collectivism* value dimension is universal.

The same argument will not work as well for the *altruism/self-interest* dimension. The position here relies on an evolutionary hypotheses; that humans, as a social species, were under selection pressure to develop a superego to control problems of in-group aggression and free riding (Boyd and Richerson 1992). Once moral sense had been selected and it became a natural human proclivity, the potential internal conflict of doing good to others versus pursuing one's things for oneself was set in place, giving rise to the *altruism/self-interest* value dimension. Again, whatever set point anyone adopts along the continuum, internal conflicts are likely to arise unless one is sociopathic or a saint.

This hypothesis potentially explains why the Baktaman have not developed personal values concerning generosity but the Balinese have. Without conflict, there is no reason to have values, personal or social. Institutionalized values are constructed to handle external conflicts, while personal values are internal defenses to handle internal conflicts. Both involve setting up some point between the poles of the opposing tendencies—some standard that says "this is just right, not too warm and not too cold." Without some conflict, one simply does as one wishes. This seems to be the case with the Baktaman. There is no conflict about selfishness because in their environment it works better to share. Given no conflict, they have no need to elaborate standards of generosity, although they like it fine when someone is generous. But the Balinese, who are the furthest eastward extension of Indic culture, have the complex conflicts about being good and giving to others versus being selfish and accumulating things for oneself typical of complex stratified societies. Hence the cultural elaboration of personal and institutionalized values of generosity.

Similarly, the Vietnamese face conflict between their disposition to achieve and the solid core of obligations to the family. The collectivist values of the Vietnamese appear to mark the line in the conflict between setting one's own goals and accepting the goals of the group further in the direction of the group than the personal value system of Americans and Japanese. But the tension between the two ends of the dimension is clearly there, as Leininger's field materials demonstrate. As Leininger and others have pointed out, the incorporation of the family as the collective from which one derives status and prestige as well as the comforts of relatedness is a good solution to the problem, but there are always tensions that even this solution cannot resolve, such as Bác Tam's wish to return to Vietnam to escape from his American *cu li* position.

The Japanese situation is different in that the conflict is externally, rather than internally, located. The quantitative data show that, like the Americans, the Japanese highly value choosing their own goals, being independent, and self-reliant, being true to oneself, having one's own point of view, and saying what one thinks (see appendix). Unlike the Chinese Confucian family, which is a source of both great value and great obligation, the Japanese family is, as described earlier by Peak, a source of relaxation and pleasure. Lacking the family as a source for internalized collective value, the Japanese rely on the same external role-based collectivist values to legitimate the high level of collaborative effort that guided them before modernization, emphasizing collectivist values in certain roles but not others.

Conclusion

The ideas with which this book finishes are different from the ideas that it started with. It now seems large differences in personal values across societies do not exist. There are some differences in personal values between societies, but there is close to overwhelming evidence that these differences are small. The variation within a society is many times larger than the variation between societies in personal values.

This does not mean that societies are all the same. First, as has been pointed out a number of times, there are large differences between societies in what-counts-as-what. The same value can be instantiated in very different ways. The canonical example is that the practices thought to give toddlers independence in a Japanese pre-school are different from the practices thought to give toddlers independence in an American preschool. There also are, it is clear, great differences in institutionalized values. The largest value differences seem to be between roles within a society, but to the degree that the same institutionalized values are found in a variety of institutions, whole societies can vary greatly with respect to institutionalized values, as exemplified by the value of purity in India.

It is difficult for people to give up using the term *value* when actually referring to *behavioral* differences. For example, after teaching students about the Fujita and Sano effect, it often happens that soon afterward a student will explain some group behavioral difference as due to a difference in values. There seems to be a wish to essentialize when some behavioral difference signals something deep and important to the observer. Given the ease of making this essentializing move that can satisfy so many ideological proclivities, it is unlikely that it will ever be popularly understood that cultures do not vary much in personal values. We do not want to believe this.

Perhaps the fact that cultures do not vary much in personal values will be taken by social scientists to indicate that there is little sense in bothering to study personal values on the group level. This conclusion would be a mistake because life satisfactions and physical health are affected by the fit between personal values and institutionalized values in important life-world institutions such as work and family (Rohan 2000, Meglino and Ravlin 1998, cited earlier). Also, differences between personal values and institutionalized values can give rise to social conflict. Of course, given sufficient external power applied to keep the social standards in place, as in slavery or in totalitarian regimes, the distress caused by lack of fit can be ignored. That is, until the day comes when it cannot be ignored.

Were I to begin the study of values now, I would focus on these questions about the degree of fit between institutionalized values and personal values. It would also be helpful to find some way of systematically surveying what-counts-as-what. Techniques to do this could be helpful in resolving cross-cultural misunderstandings. Unless one knows what-counts-as-what, one cannot understand much of political conflict. It is easy to describe the conflicts but more difficult to discover the nature of the linkages between values and the practices. What is needed is a general theory that can be used to conceptualize the psychological and cultural processes involved.

Exteriorized Values

There is another aspect of values that at least deserves mention. This book has focused on personal values and institutionalized values, but has not been concerned with the world of values that exists in cultural symbolic representations, such as movies, sermons, sacred texts, statues, plays, commencement addresses, advertisements, and the like. Following Durkheim, these can be called *collective representations*. This is the *exteriorization* of values, in which values are represented in a symbolic media that then becomes part of a cultural heritage, and in this sense these value live outside us. Symbolic media are physical artifacts such as chairs and computers, only somewhat softer—words and images on paper or film or in cyberspace, for example. One example, of a study of exteriorized values, discussed earlier, was

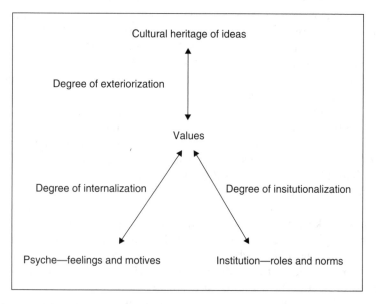

Figure 10.3 Three loci of value.

Rokeach's study of editorials in *Science*. In that case, the exteriorized values were a good indicator of institutionalized values. But, obviously, not everything in editorials is a good indicator of the social or personal values of anyone.

The study of exteriorized values faces sampling problems; there is so much value material in books, magazines, movies, blogs, and so on, that even thinking about how to sample these values is daunting. And just as daunting is the problem that, in becoming exteriorized, such values have potentially become so free of human beings that it is hard to know whether or not they have any relation to anything. The advertisements in *Town and Country* are different from the advertisements in *Wrestling Today*—each may belong to something somewhere, but what? Not necessarily to the people who read these magazines, the values embedded in the advertisements may only interest or amuse or tease the reader as possible ways of being or as the values of a kind of person who exists only in imagination. Simply coding exteriorized values sample from collective representations as a way to describe a culture seems unlikely to be useful without a theory of what is being sampled. However, when the exteriorized values can be tied in to people's personal and institutionalized values—when they are saliently used as legitimization or exemplification, for instance—they have the potential of creating strong causal effects. To be metaphoric, one can think of the exteriorized values found in collective representations as resonators—not things that can produce an effect on their own, but things that can greatly amplify an effect that is already there. For those who believe, the scripture has a powerful voice.

Final Word

A final word. It would not seem to take much intellectual effort to see that *individualism/collectivism, altruism/self-interest, and industry/ relaxation* are likely candidates for universal value dimensions. Nor is it really surprising that societies do not differ much in personal values, given both the common genetic makeup and the fact that we all share common group obligations and self-serving desires. Also, the observation that societies differ more in what-counts-as-what than in what people personally deeply value has been made by many commentators on the human scene who have remarked that customs differ more than habits of the heart. And the point that value standards can become *shoulds* institutionalized in roles is part of many social science theories.

But it was not so obvious in 1997 looking into the future as it is now in 2007 looking back into the past. If the results had turned out as I originally expected, perhaps people would have said,

> Of course—anthropologists and others have known for decades that each culture has its own unique value orientations, and that the major difference between cultures is their values. And a moment's thought shows that the differences in what-counts-as-what will always be a reflection of the basic cultural differences in values, and that personal values are always reflected in the values that are expressed in the roles we play.

Once this story seemed right. But now the evidence is against this story and it is time to construct something better.

Appendix

Four Level Taxonomy for 329 Specific Value Items

	Individualism versus collectivism		
	Americans	Japanese	Vietnamese
Individualism			
Personal exploration	Below av | Above av	Below av | Above av	Below av | Above av
Being open to change (0.6)	−1.0 −.5 0 .5 1.0	−1.0 −.5 0 .5 1.0	−1.0 −.5 0 .5 1.0
0.5 Being flexible	|====	|====:	|==
0.7 Being open to new ideas	|====:=	|====:	|=
0.7 Being open to change	|====:	|===	|
0.5 Being tolerant of different ideas and beliefs	|====:==	|====	==|
0.6 Accepting change	|====	|===	|=
0.4 Being spontaneous and open	|===	|====	=:====|
0.5 Trying out new things	|====	|===	=:====|
Being creative (0.6)			
0.7 Being creative	|====:=	|====:===	|==
0.7 Developing new ideas	|====:	|====	|===
0.4 Being interested in many things	|====:	|====:	=|
0.6 Thinking up new ways of doing things	|==	|===	|===
0.7 Being imaginative	|====:	|====:==	:====|

Continued

Appendix Table   Continued

	Americans	Japanese	Vietnamese
0.3 Catching on to things quickly	|====	|	|=
0.4 Being intuitive	|====	|	|
Understanding science (0.2)			
0.8 Understanding science	|	|=	|==
0.8 Science	=|	|=	|=
0.8 Learning scientific explanations for things	=|	|==	|=
0.6 Finding out how things work	|==	|=	===|
0.5 Seeking universal truths	=|	=|	|
Liking art and literature (0.4)			
0.6 Reading books	|===	|====:=	|=
0.8 Art (paintings, drawings, sculpture)	|==	|====	=|
0.7 Reading poetry	=:====|	==:====|	==:====:====|
0.6 Going to concerts	====:====|	:====:====|	=:====:====|
Living a life of adventure (0.6)			
0.7 Traveling to new places	|====:=	|===	=|
0.8 Living a life of adventure	|=	=:====|	=:====:====|
0.3 Taking risks	=|	====|	−1.4
0.7 Living in a different country	=:====|	:====|	:====:====|
Resisting authority (0.3)			
0.6 Questioning ideas everyone believes are true	|	==|	:====|
0.5 Limiting the power of government	:====|	====|	=:====|
0.5 Being different from others	=|	====|	:====:====|
0.5 Overthrowing political elites	−1.3	−1.6	|
0.6 Going against the crowd	====|	=:====:====|	−1.4
0.7 Resisting authority	=:====:====|	==:====|	−1.3

Continued

Appendix Table Continued

	Americans	Japanese	Vietnamese
Self-satisfactions			
Sexual freedom (0.5)			
0.7 Birth control	|=	|==	=:====|
0.7 Rights to abortion	|=	====|	=:====:====|
0.7 Sexual freedom	|=	:====|	:====:====|
0.7 Sex before marriage	==:====|	:====|	==:====:====|
0.7 Gay rights	==|	=:====|	−1.6
Being relaxed and enjoying life (0.4)			
0.6 Being relaxed	|====:=	|====:====	|
0.6 Enjoying life	|====:====:	|====:====	====|
0.5 Having time for myself	|====:=	|====:===	|
0.5 Having time to relax and take it easy	|====:=	|====:=	|==
0.5 Having comfort and contentment	|====:==	|====	==|
0.6 Taking in easy	|==	|=	|====:
0.4 Listening to music	|====	|===	===|
Having Fun (0.4)			
0.5 Having fun	|====:===	|====:===	|====:
0.7 Having a sense of humor	|====:===	|===	====|
0.7 Joking around	|===	−1.4	−1.3
Having love and a satisfying sexual life (0.3)			
0.6 Having love	|====:====	|====:====	|==
0.2 Finding a mate with good moral and intellectual quality	|====:===	|=	|====:==
0.6 Falling in love	|====:===	|====	===|
0.7 Having a satisfying sexual life	|===	|=	==:====|
0.8 Having erotic pleasure	|=	|=	===:====|
0.4 Expressing feelings physically	==|	===|	====|
Having time alone (0.3)			
0.5 Having privacy	|====:=	|====:===	|
0.4 Having peace and quiet	|==	|====:	|

Continued

	Americans	Japanese	Vietnamese
0.9 Spending time by myself	|===	|=	==|
0.8 Being alone	=:====|	=|	====:====|
Self-determination			
Choosing my own goals (0.4)			
0.5 Choosing my own goals	|====:====	|====:===	|====:=
0.2 Being independent and self-reliant	|====:===	|====:=	|====:=
0.5 Being true to myself	|====:===	|====:===	|=
0.7 Having my own point of view	|====:=	|====:==	|==
0.5 Saying what I think	|===	|===	=|
0.4 Taking the initiative	|====	===:====|	|=
Feeling sure about myself (0.4)			
0.6 Feeling sure about myself	|====:=	|====	|====
0.6 Understanding myself	|====:==	|====:==	|===
0.6 Having a positive self image	|====:=	|====:==	|
0.5 Being able to express myself well	|====:	|====:	==|
0.5 Thinking well of myself	|====:	===|	|
Self-fulfillment (0.3)			
0.5 Improving myself	|====:=	|====:==	|====:
0.5 Having a personally fulfilling life	|====:====	|====:=	|=
Being optimistic (0.3)			
0.7 Having a positive outlook on life	|====:==	|====:====	|====:
0.8 Doing what God wants me to	====:====|	−1.4	=:====|

Continued

Appendix Table   Continued

	Americans	Japanese	Vietnamese
0.8 Being optimistic	l====:	l===	l===
0.6 Seeing the best in a situation	l====	l	l=

Collectivism
Social order
  Having law and social order (−0.3)

	Americans	Japanese	Vietnamese
0.6 Law and order	=l	l===	l====:=
0.7 Government based on laws	=l	l====:	l====
0.5 Social planning	:====l	====l	l
0.5 Paying income tax	=:====:====l	===l	l====
0.5 Having a well-organized society	==l	−1.7	l===

  The military, national security, conservatism (−0.5)

	Americans	Japanese	Vietnamese
0.5 Maintaining national security	:====l	l====	l====:
0.6 The death sentence for murders	==:====l	=l	==l
0.7 Standing during the national anthem	:===l	:====:====l	l==
0.7 The military	:====:====l	−1.3	l=
0.4 Conservative political policies	−1.3	==:====:====l	−1.3

  Defending my country (−0.6)

	Americans	Japanese	Vietnamese
0.8 My country	=l	l=	l====:=
0.9 Defending my country	==:====l	=l	l====:
0.8 Being loyal to my country	:====l	:====l	l====:

Collectivism
Social order
  Being religious (−0.4)

	Americans	Japanese	Vietnamese
0.8 Having strong religious faith	====:====l	−1.6	=l
0.8 Being religious	:====:====l	==:====:====l	====l
0.7 Observing religious holidays	==:====l	−1.6	====l

Continued

Appendix Table Continued

	Americans	Japanese	Vietnamese
0.8 Being guided by religious scriptures	==:====:====|	−1.7	===:====|
Personal relations			
Being sexual restrained (−0.4)			
0.7 Not committing adultery	|====:=	|====	|====
0.8 Not sleeping around	|====	|====	|===
0.6 Being sexually modest	===|	=|	|
0.6 Virginity	==:====|	−1.3	|===
Being respectful and polite (−0.5)			
0.6 Being polite and well mannered	|====	|====:=	|====:=
0.7 Showing respect to older people	|====	|=	|====:==
0.7 Respecting superiors and showing kindness to inferior	==|	|====	|====:==
Working for the group (−0.5)			
0.6 Being obedient	=:====|	=:====|	|====
0.6 Doing what others expect me to	====:====|	:====|	|==
0.4 Going along with group decisions	====:====|	=:====|	==|
0.4 Marrying someone from my own ethnic group	−1.3	−1.3	==|
0.5 Staying where I was born and raised	−1.5	−1.5	===|
Maintaining tradition (−0.6)			
0.5 Promoting the values of my culture	===|	|=	|====:
0.3 Using firm discipline with children	===|	|====:==	====|

Continued

	Americans	Japanese	Vietnamese
0.8 Having strong traditions	===I	====I	I====:=
0.8 Maintaining old traditions	====I	==I	I====:
0.3 Remembering and honoring the past	I	=I	:====I
0.5 Preserving the family name	====I	:====:====I	I====
0.4 Taking part in ceremonies		===:====I	====I

Having a close-knit family (−0.6)

	Americans	Japanese	Vietnamese
0.7 Being close to my family	I====:==	I====:==	I====:=
0.8 Having a close-knit family	I====:=	I====:==	I====:==
0.6 Having respect for parents and grandparents	I====	I===	I====:====:
0.6 Taking care of my parents when they get older	I====	I===	I====:====
0.5 Not dishonoring my family	I	I====	I====:===
0.6 Having and raising children	I====	I==	I====:=
0.7 Fulfilling family obligations	I=	I==	I====:===
0.4 Not getting divorced	I===	:====I	I====
0.4 Taking responsibility for my siblings	==I	====I	I====:
0.5 Having big family gatherings	=I	=:====:====I	I===
0.4 Marrying someone my parents would approve of	:====I	==:====:====I	=:====I

Circumspection
Being careful (−0.4)

	Americans	Japanese	Vietnamese
0.7 Being careful to avoid mistakes	I	I==	I====
0.7 Being careful and avoiding unnecessary risks	=:====I	I	=I

Continued

	Americans	Japanese	Vietnamese
0.5 Not getting involved with someone of bad reputation	==:====|	=:====|	:====|
Being thrifty (−0.3)			
Taking good care of one's belongings	|=	|====	|==
Being thrifty	===|	|	|====
Altruism vs. self-interest			
Altruism			
Egalitarianism			
Treating people equally (0.6)			
0.7 The elimination of racism	|====:=	|====:===	|====:=
0.7 Treating people equally	|====:=	|====:==	|====:
0.4 Not having social distinctions between people	=|	|====:===	|====
0.5 Understanding people who think differently	|====	|====:=	|=
0.5 Accepting people as they are	|====:	|	|==
Respecting others' feelings (0.6)			
0.6 Showing gratitude	|====:	|====:====	|====:=
0.4 Being loyal to my friends	|====:==	|====:==	|===
0.6 Not deceiving others	|===	|====:==	|====:==
0.4 Respecting others' feelings	|====:==	|====	|====:
0.6 Respecting others' privacy	|====	|====:==	|====:
0.5 Forgiving others	|====:	|====	|====:==
0.4 Keeping secrets	|	|====:==	|====:
0.4 Being patient	|====	|==	|====
0.5 Feeling the pain of others	=|	|====:==	|==
0.3 Cooperating with others	|===	|====:	=|
Being honest and genuine (0.3)			
0.6 Following my conscience and doing right	|====:===	|====:===	|====:====

Continued

	Americans	Japanese	Vietnamese
0.8 Being honest and genuine	|====:===	|====:===	|====:==
0.6 Being a good person	|====:====:	|====:	|====:==
Having close friends (0.2)			
0.6 Having close supportive friends	|====:===	|====:====:	|==
0.5 Getting along with others	|====:=	|====:	|====:=
0.6 Having someone I can really talk to	|====:====	|====:====	=|
0.6 Making friends	|====:	|====:====:	|=
0.5 Being pleasant	|====:	|=	|====:
0.2 Having trust in others	|====:	|====:=	=|
0.1 Getting along with others through mutual concessions	|	|==	|====:
0.1 Being modest	|	|===	|===
0.3 Keeping in touch with old friends	|===	|==	=|
0.2 Taking care of others	|===	=|	|=
0.5 Being open about feelings	|====	|===	=:====|
Finding meaning in life (0.4)			
0.6 Treating human life as precious	|====:=	|====:====:=	|====:====
0.7 Finding meaning in life	|====	|====:	|====:
0.6 Coming to terms with the shortness of life	====|	:====|	|=
Social amelioration			
Working for social improvement (0.6)			
0.3 Having freedom of speech and action	|====:==	|====:=	|===
0.4 Maintaining equal opportunity for all	|====:	|==	|====:=
0.5 Improving social conditions	|==	|===	|===
0.6 Protection of minority rights	|===	|==	|==
0.6 Fighting discrimination	|==	|=	|===
0.4 Liberal political policies	====|	|	|====

Continued

	Americans	Japanese	Vietnamese
0.5 Increasing welfare for the disadvantaged	=:====|	|==	|===
0.6 Working for social justice	=|	=:====|	|====:
0.5 Feeling sympathy for those who are badly off	|	===:====|	|====
0.4 Giving to charity	|	=:====|	|=
0.4 Battling for a cause	|=	==:====|	=|
Public schools, the UN, health care (0.4)			
0.5 Democracy	|==	|====:=	|====
0.5 National health care	==|	|==	|====:
0.7 Public schools	|=	=|	=|
0.6 The United Nations	====|	|	|
0.5 Labor unions	:====:====|	===:====|	=:====|
Altruism			
Egalitarianism			
Avoiding war (0.4)			
0.5 Avoiding war	|====	|====:====:==	|====:==
0.5 Having a world free of war	|====	|====:====:	|====:=
Living in harmony with nature (0.5)			
0.5 Maintaining a sustainable environment	|=	|====:===	|====
0.7 Protecting the environment	|==	|====:==	|===
0.7 Enjoying the beauty of nature	|====	|====:	|=
0.7 Living in harmony with nature	|==	|====:=	|==
0.6 Being close to nature	|	|====:=	===|
0.7 Having emotional ties with the natural environment	==|	===|	==|

Continued

	Americans	Japanese	Vietnamese
Personal adjustment (0.3)			
Being able to adjust (0.3)			
0.3 Being able to adjust	|====:==	|====	|===
0.5 Admitting my mistakes	|==	|====:==	|====
0.2 Gaining experience and wisdom from suffering	==|	|====:==	|====
0.6 Living in the present	|==	|====:	|
0.7 Being a good loser	|	|====	|=
0.3 Being patient and resigned when misfortunes occur	===|	|=	|===
0.5 Laughing at difficulties	=|	|	==:====:====|
Controlling myself (0.2)			
0.6 Having self-control	|====:	|====:	|====:
0.3 Having self-discipline	|====:=	|===	|====
0.6 Thinking before speaking	|==	|==	|====:
0.6 Keeping one's cool	|=	|==	|==
0.6 Overcoming temptation	|	|=	|==
0.6 Not losing my temper	|=	|===	===|
0.5 Keeping my emotions under control	|	==|	=|
0.4 Not overindulging	===|	=:====|	==|
0.1 Minding my own business	==|	|=	=:====:====|
Self-interest			
Success			
Being prosperous (−0.5)			
0.5 Having a secure job	|====	|==	|====:==
0.5 Being employed	|====	|=	|====:===

Continued

	Americans	Japanese	Vietnamese
0.2 Staying out of debt	|====:	|===	|===
0.2 Saving money in case of an emergency	|==	|==	|====:=
0.6 Having financial security	|====	|===	|==
0.7 Not being poor	|=	|	|=
0.6 Being prosperous	|	==|	|===
0.3 Having business skills	==|	=|	|==
0.6 Making good a profit	====|	==:====|	====|
0.6 Having great wealth	==:====|	:====:====|	|=
Having social status (−0.07)			
0.1 Being with people who feel about things the way	|	=|	|==
0.6 Being important	==|	=:====|	=:====|
0.7 Having social status	=:====|	===:====|	:====|
0.6 Being one of the elite	===:====|	:====:====|	:====|
0.6 Being the center of attention	:====:====|	==:====:====|	====:====|
0.7 Being famous	−1.5	−1.3	====:=====|
Having nice things, good looks, taste, success(−0.7)			
0.5 Having good taste	|	|=====	|==
0.3 Having a leisurely lifestyle	|	|====	==|
0.5 Being a success	|===	=:=====|	|===
0.3 getting my own way	===|	==|	|=
0.2 Being protected	|	==|	:=====|
0.4 Having someone who will take care of me	===|	==|	=:=====|
Self-interest			
Success			
Having nice things, good looks, etc.			
0.6 Being well dressed	====|	|=	====:====|

Continued

Appendix Table   Continued

	Americans	Japanese	Vietnamese
0.6 Having good looks	====|	=:====|	===|
0.3 Having a rich fantasy life	=:====|	|=	==:====|
0.7 Owning a good stereo, a nice car, house	:====|	=:====|	====:====|
0.4 Having authority over others	=:====:====|	−1.3	===:====|
0.4 Paying others back for insults and injuries	==:====:====|	−1.3	−1.5
Self-advancement			
Being ambitious and competitive (−0.5)			
0.6 Wanting to amount to something special	|====:	:====|	====|
0.7 Being ambitious	|===	====|	==:====|
0.7 Being competitive	====|	=|	====|
Market competition, economic growth, capitalism (−0.2)			
0.7 Economic growth	====|	|	|====:
0.6 Capitalism	==:====|	=|	=|
0.7 Market competition	====:====|	===|	===|
Keeping fit (−0.3)			
0.7 Being healthy	|====:===	|====:====:===	|====:===
0.7 Exercising and keeping fit	|==	|====:===	|==
0.6 Having a long life	|==	===|	|
0.5 Having a good physique	=|	:====|	====|
0.3 Dieting	==:====:====|	|====	:====:====|

Continued

	Americans	Japanese	Vietnamese
Acceptance			
Being liked and belonging (−0.4)			
0.7 Being liked	|=	|=	|
0.5 Having a good reputation	|=	|	|=
0.5 Fitting in	==:====|	|==	|====:
0.6 Being approved of	===|	|==	|=
0.6 Having others think well of me	|==	====|	=|
0.5 Not losing face	===|	===|	|===
0.6 Feeling that one belongs	=|	==:====|	|=
0.4 Being part of a group	===|	=:====|	===:====|
In industry			
Striving			
Having high standards (0.6)			
0.5 Developing ability and skill	|====:==	|====:==	|===
0.7 Being competent and effective	|====:==	|===	|====:
0.7 Holding myself to high standards	|====:==	|=	|====:
0.2 Facing problems directly	|====	|====:	|====
0.7 Maintaining high standards	|====:	|=	|=
0.2 Trying to be the best	|	===:====|	==|
Pursuing knowledge and being well informed (0.3)			
0.7 Pursuing knowledge	|====:==	|====:==	|====:
0.4 Having wisdom	|====:===	|====:	|==
0.5 Knowing the facts	|====	|====:===	|==
0.5 Being intelligent	|====:===	|==	|===
0.2 Seeking explanations	|===	|=	|==
0.5 Having a good vocabulary	|==	|====	|=

Continued

	Americans	Japanese	Vietnamese
0.5 Knowing what's going on in the world	|==	|====:=	==|
0.6 Being well informed	|====	|====	===|
0.1 Getting things to add up	|	===|	|====
Being a leader (0.3)			
0.6 Good leadership	|===	=|	|====:
0.5 Being able to influence what happens	|===	===|	====|
0.5 Being able to run things the way I want	==|	===:====|	=|
0.4 Organization and coordinating activities	:====|	===:====|	|=
0.8 Being a leader	=|	===:====|	:====|
Diligence			
Being persistent (0.6)			
0.6 Being persistent	|====:	|====:===	|====:
0.5 Having will power	|====:=	|====:===	|====
0.5 Not giving up hope	|====:==	|====:===	|==
0.7 Not giving up	|====:=	|====:=	|==
0.4 Persevering to overcome difficulties	|====:	|==	|====:=
0.4 Finishing what one starts	|====	|====:	|====
Working hard (0.6)			
0.7 Working hard	|====:==	|====:=	|====:=
0.6 Getting things done	|====:	|====:	|====:
0.7 Completing work on time	|====	==|	|====:=
0.4 Being busy	==|	===:====|	:====|
Being orderly and regular (0.5)			
0.5 Being punctual	|=	|====:==	|====:
0.4 Being prepared	|====	|	|===

Continued

	Americans	Japanese	Vietnamese
0.4 Paying attention to details	|===	|====	==|
0.5 Doing things in logical order	|	|=	|===
0.6 Being orderly and regular	==|	|=	|====
0.5 Keeping things tidy	=|	|=	|==
0.2 Being exact	====|	|==	|==
0.5 Getting tasks done right away	=|	|	|
0.1 Having a work routine	=|	===|	====:====|
Being responsibility (0.4)			
0.8 Being responsible	|====:===	|====:==	|====:===
0.4 Being reliable	|====:==	|====:====	|====:=
0.7 Taking responsibility for decisions	|====:==	|====:==	|====:=
0.5 Fulfilling my obligations	|===	|====:	|====:==
−0.1 Being able to follow orders	===|	==:====|	|
Canniness			
Planning for the future (0.3)			
0.6 The future	|====:	|====:====	|====:==
0.7 Thinking about the future	|====:	|====:=	|====:
0.6 Planning for the future	|====:	|==	|====:
0.4 Thinking ahead	|===	=|	|==
Being practical and realistic (0.2)			
−0.1 Knowing my own strengths and weaknesses	|====:=	|====:=	|====
0.8 Being practical	|==	|==	|===
0.8 Being realistic	|===	|==	|===
Relaxation			
Amusements			
Enjoying comics, board games, sports (−0.3)			
0.5 Playing and watching sports	=:====|	=|	:====|

Continued

	Americans	Japanese	Vietnamese
0.7 Reading comics	−1.5	=:====:====|	−1.3
0.7 Playing board games (checkers, Monopoly, etc.)	−1.4	−2.0	−1.5
Watching movies, tv, eating out (−0.3)			
0.8 Going to movies	===|	===|	:====:====|
0.7 Watching TV	=:====:====|	=:====|	==:====|
0.8 Eating in restaurants	:====|	====:====|	==:==:====|
Sleeping, eating, drinking alcohol (−0.04)			
0.7 Sleeping	|====:	|====:===	|==
0.8 Eating	|=	|====:==	==|
0.5 Drinking alcohol	=:====:====|	===:====|	−1.7
Disegagements			
Being detached and accepting one's fate (−0.2)			
0.2 Being reserved and acting with discretion	===|	==|	|====:
0.5 Learning to accept what can't be changed	|	|	|=
0.6 Accepting one's fate	====|	==|	:====|
0.5 Not pursuing unattainable dreams	=:====:====|	===:====|	==|
0.4 Depreciating myself and complimenting others	====:====|	:====:====|	====|
0.4 Staying out of politics	===:====|	:====:====|	:====:====|
0.4 Not standing out from others	−1.4	−1.3	===:====|
0.6 Being detached from what happens in the world	−1.4	−1.3	−1.2
Believing in omens, mysticism, dreams, psychics (−0.3)			
0.6 Remembering my dreams	=|	|====:==	=:====:====|
0.5 Being lucky	====|	|=	=:====|
0.6 Having mystical experiences	====:====|	=:====:====|	====|
0.7 Paying attention to omens	−1.3	===|	==:====|

Continued

Appendix Table   Continued

	Americans	Japanese	Vietnamese
0.5 Consulting psychics	−2.0	−2.1	−1.6
Unclassified			
Getting along with my spouse's family and friend	|====	|====:=	n.d.
Taking the viewpoint of others	====|	|====:==	|
Working for group consensus	====|	=|	|===
Knowing my place in the social order	==:====:====|	====|	==|
Taking in stray animals	===:====|	====:====|	====:====|
Loafing	=:====:====|	:====:====|	n.d.
Conquering nature	−1.6	−1.4	====|
Living the life of a farmer	−1.7	−1.4	==:====:====|

Bibliography

Aldenderfer, Mark S. and Roger K. Blashfield. 1984. *Cluster Analysis*. Beverly Hills: Sage.

Allport, Gordon W. 1960. *The Study of Value: A Scale for Measuring the Dominant Interests in Personality*. New York: Houghton Miffin.

Allport, Gordon W., P. E. Vernon, and G. Lindzey. 1966. *The Nature of Prejudice*. New York: Addison-Wesley.

Arrindell, W. A., C. Hatzichristou, J. Wensink, E. Rosenberg, B. van Twillert, J. Stedema, and D. Meijer. 1997. Dimensions of national culture as predictors of cross-national differences in subjective well-being. *Personality and Individual Differences* 23: 37–53.

Baron, H. 1996. Strengths and limitations of ipsative measurement. *Journal of Occupational and Organizational Psychology* 69: 48–57.

Barth, Fredrick. 1993. Are values real? In *The Origin of Values*, Michael Hecter, Lynn Nadel, and Richard E. Michod, eds. New York: Aldine.

Benedict, Ruth. 1945. *The Chrysanthemum and the Sword*. New York: Houghton and Mifflin.

Bertam, D. 1996. The relationship between ipsatized and normative measures of personality. *Journal of Occupational and Organizational Psychology* 69: 25–41.

Borg, I. and J. C. Lingoes. 1987. *Multidimensional Similarity Structure Analysis*. New York: Springer-Verlag.

Boster, James. n.d. The value of cognitive diversity: The correlation of local aggregates with World Standards. Unpublished manuscript.

———. 1987. Intracultural variation. *American Behavioral Scientist* Special Issue 31: 2.

Boyd, R. and P. J. Richerson. 1992. Punishment allows the evolution of cooperation (or anything else) in sizable groups. *Ethnology and Sociobiology* 13: 171–195.

Bruner, J. S., J. J. Goodnow, and G. A. Austin. 1956. *A Study of Thinking*. New York: John Wiley.

Burton, M., E. Greenberger, and C. Hayward. 2005. Mapping the ethnic landscape: Personal beliefs about own group's and other groups' traits. *Cross-Cultural Research* 39(4): 351.

Cancian, Francesca. 1975. *What Are the Norms?* New York: Cambridge University Press.

Caplan, N. S., M. H. Choy, and J. K. Whitmore. 1989. *The Boat People and Achievement in America: A Study of Family Life, Hard Work, and Cultural Values*. Ann Arbor, MI: University of Michigan Press.

Caplan, N. S., M. H. Choy, and J. K. Whitmore. 1991. *Children of the Boat People: A Study of Educational Success*. Ann Arbor, MI: University of Michigan Press.

Carstairs, M. 1957. *The Twice Born*. Bombay: Allied Publishers.

Cattell, R. B. and J. Brennan. 1994. Finding personality structure when ipsative measurements are the unavoidable basis of the variables. *American Journal of Psychology* 107: 261–274.

Caudill, William and David W. Plath. 1966. Who sleeps by whom? *Psychiatry* 29: 344–366.

Cohen, J. 1988. *Statistical Power Analysis for the Behavioral Sciences*, 2nd. ed. Hillside, NJ: Lawrence Earlbaum Associates.

Comrey, Andrew and Howard Lee. 1992. *A First Course in Factor Analysis*, 2nd. ed. Hillsdale: Erlbaum.

Costa, P. T. Jr. and R. R. McCrae. 1994. Stability and change in personality from adolescence through adulthood. *In The Developing Structure of Temperament and Personality from Infancy to Adulthood*, C. F. Halverson, G. A. Kohnstamm, and R. Martin, eds., pp. 139–150. Hillsdale, NJ: L. Earlbaum Associates.

Cronbach, Lee J. Coefficient alpha and the internal structure of tests. *Psychometrica* 16(3): 297–334.

D'Andrade, Roy. 1995. *The Development of Cognitive Anthropology*. Cambridge: Cambridge University Press.

———. 2006. Commentary on Searle's "Social ontology: Some basic principles": Culture and institutions. *Anthropological Theory* 6(1): 30–39.

Diener, Ed, Marissad Diener, and Carol Diener. 1995. Components predicting the subjective well-being of nations. *Journal of Personality and Social Psychology* 69(5): 851–864.

Dore, Ronald P. 1978. *Shinohata: A Portrait of a Japanese Village*. New York: Pantheon Books.

Dubois, Cora. 1955. The dominant value profile of American culture. *American Anthropologist* 57: 1232–1239.

Dumont, Louis. 1980. *Homo Hierarchicus: The Caste System and Its Implications*. Revised English Edition, Chicago: University of Chicago Press.

Dunlap, William P. and John M. Cornwell. 1994. Component analysis of ipsative measures. *Multivariate Behavioral Research* 29(1): 115–126.

Edmonson, Munro S. The Anthropology of values. *In Culture and Life*, W. W. Taylor, J. L. Fischer, and E. Z. Vogt, eds. Carbondale: Southern Illinois University Press.

Fiorina, Morris P., Samuel J. Abrams, and Jeremy C. Pope. *Culture War? 2005. The Myth of a Polarized America*. New York: Longman.

Freeman, J. M. 1989. *Hearts of Sorrow: Vietnamese-American Lives*. Stanford, CA: Stanford University Press.

———. *Changing Identities: Vietnamese Americans, 1975–1995*. Boston: Allyn and Bacon.

Fujita, Mariko and Toshiyuki Sano. 1988. Children in American and Japanese day-care centers. In *School and Society*, H. T. Trueba and C. Delgado-Gaitan, eds. New York: Praeger.

Gillin, John. 1955. National and regional cultural values in the United States. *Social Forces* 34: 107–113.

Goldberg, L. R. 1999. A broad-bandwidth, public-domain, personality inventory measuring the lower-level facets of several five-component models. *In Personality Psychology in Europe. Volume 7*, I. Mervielde, I. J. Deary, F. De Fruyt, and F. Ostendorf. Tilburg, eds., pp. 7–28. The Netherlands: Tilburg University Press.

Goldberg, Lewis R. and John M. Digman. 1994. Revealing structure in the data: Principles of exploratory component analysis. In *Differentiating Normal and Abnormal Personality*, S. Strack and M. Lorr, eds., pp. 216–242. New York: Springer.

Graeber, David. 2001. *Toward an Anthropological Theory of Value*. New York: Palgrave.

Greenacre, J. M. 1993. *Correspondence Analysis in Practice*. New York: Academic Press.

Guilford, J. P. 1936. *Psychometric Methods*. New York: McGraw-Hill.

Haring, Douglas. 1949. Japanese national character: Cultural anthropology, psychoanalysis, and history. In *Personal Character and Cultural Milieu*. D. Haring, ed. Syracuse: Syracuse University Press.

Heine, Steven J., Shinobu Kitayama, Durrin Lehman, Toshitake Takata, Eugene Ide. 2001. Divergent consequences of success and failure in Japan and North America: An investigation of self-improving motivations and malleable selves. *Journal of Personality and Social Psychology* 81(4): 599–615.

Hofstede, G. 1980. *Culture's Consequences*. Beverly Hills: Sage.

Inglehart, Ronald. 1997. *Modernization and Postmodernization: Cultural, Economic, and Political Change in 43 Societies*. Princeton: Princeton University Press.

Kashima, Yoshihisa, Susumu Yamaguchi, Uichol Kim, Sand-Chin Choi, Michele Gelfand, and Masaki Yuki. 1995. Culture, gender and self: A perspective from individualism-collectivism research. *Journal of Personality and Social Psychology* 69(5): 925–937.

Keesing, Roger. 1974. Theories of culture. *Annual Reviews in Anthropology* 3: 73–97.

Kendler, Kenneth S., Xia-Quing Liu, Charles O. Gardner, Michael E. McCullough, David Larson, and Carol A. Prescott. 2003. Dimensions of religiosity and their relationship to lifetime psychiatric and substance use disorder. *American Journal of Psychiatry* 160(3): 496–503.

Kerlinger, Fred N. 1984. *Liberalism and Conservatism: The Nature and Structure of Social Attitudes*. Hillsdale:Earlbaum.

Kibria, N. 1993. *Family Tightrope: The Changing Lives of Vietnamese Americans*. Princeton, NJ: Princeton University Press.

Kitayama, Shinobu. 2002. Culture and basic psychological processes—Toward a system view of culture: Comment on Oyserman et al. *Psychological Bulletin* 12(1): 89–96.

Kitayama, Shinobu and Hazel Rose Markus. 1999. Yin and yanf of the Japanese self: The cultural psychology of personality coherence. In *The Coherence of Personality: Social Cognitive Bases of Personality Consistency, Variability, and Organization*, D. Cervone and Y. Shoda, eds. New York: Guilford.

Kitayama, Shinobu, Hazel Rose Markus, and M. Kurokawa. 2000. Culture, emotion and well-being: Good feelings in Japan and the United States. *Cognition and Emotion* 14: 93–124.

Kitayama, Shinobu, Hazel Rose Markus, Hisaya Matsumoto, and Vinai Norasakunkit. 1997. Individual and collective processes in the construction of the self: Self-enhancement in the United States and self-criticism in Japan. *Journal of Personality and Social Psychology* 72(6): 1245–1267.

Kluckhohn, Florence. 1950. Dominant and substitute profiles of cultural orientation: Their significance for the analysis of social stratification. *Social Forces* 28: 376–393.

Kluckhohn, Clyde. 1951a. Values and value-orientations in the theory of action. *In Toward a General Theory of action*, T. Parsons and E. A. Shils, eds. Cambridge, MA: Harvard University Press.

———. 1951b. A comparative study of values in five cultures. Foreword in Navaho veterans, a study in changing values, by Evon Z. Vogt. *Papers of the Peabody Museum of American Archaeology and Ethnology* 41(1): vii–ix.

———. 1958. The evolution of contemporary American values. *Daedalus* 87: 78–109.

Lebra, Takai S. 1976. *Japanese Patterns of Behavior.* Honolulu: University of Hawaii Press.

Leininger, A. 2001. *Culture and Cognitive Psychodynamics in Vietnamese-American Families.* Unpublished Doctoral Dissertation, University of California, San Diego.

———. 2002. Vietnamese-American personality and Acculturation. In *The Five Component Model Across Cultures,* R. R. McCrae and J. Allik, eds., pp. 1–23. Netherlands: Kluwer Academic Publishers.

Leung, K. and M. K. Bond. 1998. On the empirical identification of dimensions for cross-cultural comparison. *Journal of Cross-Cultural Psychology* 20(2): 133–151.

Lidz, Victor. 1991. The American value system: A commentary on Talcott Parsons's perspective and understanding. In *Talcott Parsons: Theorist of Modernity*, Roland Robertson and Bryan S. Turner, eds. London: Sage Publications.

Marriot, McKim. 1990. *India through Hindu Categories.* Newbury Park: Sage.

Mathews, Gordon. 1966. *What Makes Life Worth Living.* Berkeley: University of California Press.

McCrae, R. R. and J. Allik, eds. 2002. *The Five Component Model of Personality across Cultures.* New York: Kluwer Academic/Plenum.

McCrae, R. R. and P. T. Jr. Costa. 1997a. Conceptions and correlates of openness to experience. *In Handbook of Personality Psychology,* R. Hogan, J. A. Johnson, and S. R. Briggs, eds., pp. 825–847. San Diego, CA: Academic Press.

———. 1997b. Personality trait structure as a human universal. *American Psychologist.* 525: 509–516.

———. 1999. A five-component theory of personality. *In Handbook of Personality: Theory and Research,* 2nd ed., L. A. Pervin and O. P. John, eds., pp. 139–153. New York: Guilford Press.

McCrae, R. R., P. T. Jr. Costa, G. H. Del Pilar, J.-P. Rolland, and W. D. Parker. 1998. Cross-cultural assessment of the five-component model: The revised NEO personality inventory. *Journal of Cross-Cultural Psychology* 291: 171–188.

McCrae, R. R., M. S. M. Yik, P. D. Trapnell, M. H. Bond, and D. L. Paulhus. 1998. Interpreting personality profiles across cultures: Bilingual, acculturation, and peer rating studies of Chinese undergraduates. *Journal of Personality and Social Psychology* 744: 1041–1055.

McClelland, David C. 1951. *Personality.* New York: William Sloane.

McClelland, David C., R. Koestner, and J. Weinberger. 1989. How do self-attributed and implicit motives differ? *Psychological Review* 96(4): 690–702.

Meglino, Bruce M. and Elizabeth C. Ravlin. 1998. Individual values in organizations: Concepts, controversies, and research. *Journal of Management* 24(3): 351–389.

Minami, Yasusuke. 2005. Identity and social structure: Two socialization practices in Japanese schools. *The Seijo University Arts and Literature Quarterly* 189: 125–150.

Moore, Carmella C., A. K. Romney, Ti-lien Hsia, and Craig D. Rusch. 1999. The universality of the semantic structure of emotion terms: Methods for the study of inter- and intra-cultural variability. *American Anthropologist* 101(3): 1–18.

Nakane, Chie. 1970. *Japanese Society.* Berkeley: University of California Press.

Oishi, Shigehiro, Ulrich Schimmack, Ed Diener, and Eunkook M. Suh. 1998. The measurement of values and individualism-collectivism. *Personality and Social Psychology Bulletin* 24(11): 1177–1189.

Ornstein, Norman, Andrew Kohut, and Larry McCarthy. 1988. *The People, the Press, & Politics.* New York: Addison-Wesley.

Osgood, Charles, William May, and Murray Miron, 1975. *Cross-Cultural Universals of Affective Meaning.* Urbana: University of Illinois Press.

Oyserman, Daphna, Heather Coon, and Markus Kemmelmeier. 2002. Rethinking individualism and collectivism: Evaluation of theoretical assumptions and meta-analyses. *Psychological Bulletin* 128: 3–72.

Parsons, Talcott. 1964. *Social Structure and Personality*. New York: The Free Press.

Parsons, Talcott and Winston White. 1964. The link between character and society. In *Social Structure and Personality*, Talcott Parsons, ed. New York: Free Press.

Peak, Lois. 2001. Learning to become part of the group. In *Japanese Frames of Mind*, Hidetata Shimizu and Robert A. Levine, eds. Cambridge: Cambridge University Press.

Rankin, W. L. and J. W. Grube. 1980. A comparison of ranking and rating procedures for value measurement systems. *European Journal of Social Psychology* 10: 233–246.

Roccas, Sonia, Lilach Sagiv, Shalom H. Schwartz, and Ariel Knafo. 2002. The big five personality components and personal values. *Personality and Social Psychology Bulletin* 28(6): 789–801.

Rohan, Meg J. 2000. A rose by any name? The values construct. *Personality and Social Psychology Review* 4(3): 255–277.

Rokeach, Milton. 1967. *Value Survey*. Palo Alto: Consulting Psychologists Press.

———. 1969. Value systems in religion. *Review of Religious Research* 11: 24–38.

———. 1973. *The Nature of Human Values*. New York: Free Press.

———. 1979. From individual to supra-individual values: With special reference to the values of Science. *In Understanding Human Values*, M. Rokeach, ed. New York: Free Press.

Rokeach, Milton and Sandra J. Ball-Rokeach, 1989. Stability and change in American value priorities, 1968–1981. *American Psychologist* 44(5): 775–784.

Rokeach, Milton, Martin G. Miller, and John A. Snyder. 1971. The value gap between police and policed. *Journal of Social Issues* 27(2): 155–171.

Romney, A. K. 1989. Quantitative models, science and cumulative knowledge. *Journal of Quantitative Anthropology* 1: 153–223.

Romney, A. K., Carmella C. Moore, and Graig D. Rusch. 1997. Cultural universals: Measuring the semantic structure of emotion terms in English and Japanese. *Proceeding of the National Academy of Sciences* 94: 5489–5494.

Romney, A. Kimball, Carmella C. Moore, and Timothy J. Brazill. 1999. Correspondence analysis as a multidimensional scaling technique for non-frequency similarity matrices. In *Visualization of Categorical Data*, M. Greenacre and J. Blasius, eds. San Diego: Academic Press.

Romney, Kimball, Susan C. Weller, and William H. Batchelder. 1986. Culture as consensus. *American Anthropologist* 88 (2): 313–338.

Rumbaut, R. G. 1985. Mental health and the refugee experience: A comparative study of Southeast Asian refugees. In *Southeast Asian Mental Health: Treatment, Prevention, Services, Training, and Research*, T. C. Owan, ed., pp. 433–486. National Institute of Mental Health.

———. Portraits, patterns, and predictors of the refugee adaptation process: Results and reflections from the IHARP panel study. In *Refugees as Immigrants: Cambodians, Laotians, and Vietnamese in America*, D. W. Haines, ed., pp. 138–182. Totowa, NJ: Rowman & Littlefield Publishers, Inc.

———. 1991. The agony of exile: A study of the migration and adaptation of Indochinese refugee adults and children. In *Refugee Children: Theory, Research, and Services*, F. L. Ahearn and J. L. Athey, eds., pp. 53–91. Baltimore, MD: Johns Hopkins University Press.

Sagiv, Lilach and Shalom H. Schwartz. 2000. Value priorities and subjective well-being: direct relations and congruity effects. *European Journal of Social Psychology* 30: 177–198.

Sax, L. J., A. W. Astin, J. A. Lindholm, W. W. Korn, V. B. Saenz, and K. M. Mahoney. 2003. *The American Freshman: National Norms for Fall 2003*. Higher Education Research Institute, UCLA Graduate School of Education and Information Studies, Los Angeles.

Schimmack, Oishi and Diener 2004. Individualism: A valid and important dimension of cultural differences between nations. *Personality and Social Psychology Review* 9(1): 17–31.

Schwartz, Barry. 1993. On the creation and destruction of value. In *The Origin of Values*, Michael Hechter, Lynn Nadel, and Richard E. Michod, eds. Hawthorne, NY: Aldine.

Schwartz, Shalom, H. 1992. Universals in the content and structure of values: Theory and empirical tests in 20 countries. In *Advances in Experimental Social Psychology*, M. Zanna, ed., 25: 1–65. New York: Academic Press.

———. 2002. Mapping and interpreting cultural differences around the world. In *Comparing Cultures, Dimensions of Culture in a Comparative Perspective*, H. Vinken, J. Soeters, and P. Esters, eds. Leiden, The Netherlands: Brill.

Schwartz, Shalom, H. and Anat Bardi. 2001. Value hierarchies across cultures: Taking a similarities perspective. *Journal of Cross Cultural Psychology* 32(3): 268–290.

Schwartz, Shalom, H. and Spike Huismans. 1995. Value priorities and religiosity in four western religions. *Social Psychology Quarterly* 58(2): 88–107.

Schwartz, Shalom H., Markku Verkasalo, Avishai Antonovsky, and Lilach Sagiv. 1997. Value priorities and social desirability. *British Journal of Social Psychology* 38: 3–18.

Shimizu, Hidetada. 2000. Japanese cultural psychology and empathetic understanding: Implications for academic and cultural psychology. *Ethos* 28(2): 224–247.

Shimizu, Hidetada. 2001. Beyond individualism and sociocentrism. In *Japanese Frames of Mind*, Hidetata Shimizu and Robert A. Levine, eds. Cambridge: Cambridge. Smith, Peter B. 2004. Nations, cultures, and individuals. *Journal of Cross-Cultural Psychology* 35(1): 6–12.

Spindler, George. 1955. Education in a transforming American culture. *Harvard Educational Review* 25: 145–156.

Spiro, Melford E. 1987. *Culture and Human Nature*. Chicago: University of Chicago Press.

Strauss, Claudia, 2000. The culture concept and the individualism/collectivism debate: Dominant and alternative attributions for class in the United States. In *Culture, Thought, and Development*, Larry Nucci, Geoffrey Saxe, and Elliot Turiel, eds., pp. 85–114. Mahwah, NJ: Lawrence Erlbaum Associates.

Takano, Yohtaro and Eiko Osaka. 1999. An unsupported common view: Comparing Japan and the U.S. on individualism/collectivism. *Asian Journal of Social Psychology* 2: 311–341.

Traweek, Sharon. 1988. *Beamtimes and LifeTimes*. Cambridge: Harvard University Press.

Triandis, Harry C. 1990. Cross-cultural studies of individualism and collectivism. In *Nebraska Symposium on Motivation*, J. Berman, ed., pp. 41–133. Lincoln, NE: University of Nebraska Press.

———. 1994. *Culture and Social Behavior*. New York: McGraw-Hill.

Vogel, Ezra F. 1979. *Japan as Number 1*. Cambridge: Harvard University Press.

Vogt, Evon Z. 1955. *Modern Homesteaders*. Cambridge: Harvard University Press.

Vogt, Evon Z. and Ethel M. Albert, eds. 1966. *People of Rimrock: A Study of Values in Five Cultures*. Cambridge: Harvard University Press.

Weller, Susan C. and A. K. Romney. 1990. *Metric Scaling: Correspondence Analysis*. Newbury Park: Sage.

Werner, O. and D. T. Campbell. 1970. Translating, working through interpreters, and the problem of decentering. In *A Handbook of Method in Cultural Anthropology*, R. Naroll and R. Cohen, eds., pp. 398–420. Garden City, NY: The Natural History Press.

Williams, Robin. 1951. *American Society*. New York: Knopf.

Zhou, M. and C. L. Bankston. 1994. Social capital and the adaptation of the second generation: The case of Vietnamese youth in New Orleans. *The International Migration Review* 28: 821–839.

———. 1998. *Growing up American: How Vietnamese Children Adapt to Life in the United States*. New York: Russell Sage Foundation.

Index

Also by the Author (Books and Edited Collections)

"Schemas and Motivation," in *Human Motives and Cultural Models,* R. D'Andrade and C. Strauss (eds.), 1992.

The Development of Cognitive Anthropology, 1995.

Special Editor, *Anthropological Theory*, Volume 6(1): 2006, Special Issue on John Searle's contribution to the social sciences.